TO TVE & DEE –

Darrell Smith
Eph. 2:8

"If you want to be truly effective in every realm of your life, embrace the life-changing message within these pages. Let David Jeremiah inspire and encourage you."

—KEN BLANCHARD/Co-author of *The One Minute Manager* and *The Secret*

"Dr. Jeremiah has captured the subject of grace in a unique, practical and powerful way. When you read it, your heart, too, will be captured by grace."

—DR. TONY EVANS/Senior Pastor of Oak Cliff Bible Fellowship and President of The Urban Alternative

"I am really glad you picked up this book. *Captured by Grace* is the life-changing story of God's incredible favor and faithfulness. As always, David Jeremiah communicates with infectious joy and contagious faith. I promise that when you finish reading this book, you will say Grace really is amazing!"

—DR. JACK GRAHAM/Pastor of Prestonwood Baptist Church

"*Captured by Grace* is one of the most interesting and compelling books I have ever read. It is built on the foundation of Scripture and illustrated by the fascinating similarities between the first-century murderer Paul of Tarsus and the eighteenth-century slave trader John Newton. . . . Its unique writing style illustrates the author's incredible grasp of both Scripture and the lives of many who have been touched by the supernatural grace of God. Everyone can benefit by reading this enjoyable book."

—TIM LaHAYE/Pastor and Author

"David Jeremiah is a modern-day treasure. With his emphasis on biblical truth and close watch on the pulse of contemporary culture, Dr. Jeremiah skillfully unfolds what the grace of God is and isn't in his newest book. This is must reading for anyone who wants to walk closely with the Lord and see lasting changes in their life. I highly recommend it."

—GREG LAURIE/Senior Pastor of
Harvest Christian Fellowship

"In *Captured by Grace*, David Jeremiah offers a fresh perspective on a familiar subject and has thrown a lifeline to those who can't seem to forgive themselves, laboring under a load of guilt because they just don't feel they 'deserve' God's forgiveness. Like the brilliance of a priceless jewel that appears even more glorious when displayed on black velvet, Dr. Jeremiah describes God's grace as most vividly revealed against the backdrop of a sin-blackened life. Using the stories of John Newton and the apostle Paul as the 'black velvet,' he unveils the timeless jewel of God's grace. Read this book, and be recaptured . . . *by Him.*"

—ANNE GRAHAM LOTZ/Evangelist, Bible Teacher,
Founder of AnGeL Ministries, and Author

"It's not 'new' we need—it's fresh reminders of timeless truths. *Captured by Grace* is pure water for thirsty souls. Let David Jeremiah unplug the fountain of God's abundant grace 'til your soul is overflowing."

—JAMES MACDONALD/Pastor of Harvest Bible Fellowship
and Speaker on *Walk in the Word* Radio Program

"A compelling, vivid read—winsomely honest about how grace transforms us from victims to victors. *Captured by Grace* could just be the fresh experience of the love of God you've been waiting for."

—JOHN C. MAXWELL/Author, Speaker, and Founder of
INJOY Stewardship Services and EQUIP

"David Jeremiah reminds us that God is on the offensive. He does not wait for us to come to Him. He pursues us until we are finally captured by His grace. If you're looking for a weak and passive God, you'll not find Him in this book."

—CHRIS MORTENSEN/ESPN Analyst and Reporter

"*Captured by Grace* makes it very clear that when we accept and then experience God's loving forgiveness in our lives, it produces harmony within our relationships and repairs the hurts of our past. Regardless of our individual journey, we all need this book and the true hope it offers."

—GARY SMALLEY/Founder and CEO of the
Smalley Relationship Center

"The song that I have been performing for years, and that we Americans have come to love, takes on even deeper meaning with this powerful book. You'll never hear 'Amazing Grace' in the same way again."

—JOHN TESH/Entertainer and TV Personality

"I have read every book David Jeremiah has written and assure you that this is the most compelling."

—PAT WILLIAMS/Author and Senior Vice
President of the Orlando Magic

"Rich in illustration, gentle in its touch and profound in its implications, David Jeremiah's *Captured by Grace* addresses a timeless theme with timely relevance."

—RAVI ZACHARIAS/Christian Apologist, Author, and Teacher

CAPTURED *by*
GRACE

*No One is Beyond the Reach
of a Loving God*

"Amazing Grace"
LYRICS BY JOHN NEWTON,
WORDS FROM THE APOSTLE PAUL...
BOTH MEN...

CAPTURED by
GRACE

*No One is Beyond the Reach
of a Loving God*

DAVID JEREMIAH

INTEGRITY®
PUBLISHERS
Nashville
www.integritypublishers.com

To the people of Shadow Mountain,
who for twenty-five years have made our church a place of grace.

CONTENTS

ACKNOWLEDGMENTS

Captured by Grace is not just the title of this book. It is the phrase that best describes what has happened to all of us who have worked on this project.

The possibility of marrying the message of grace to the life stories of John Newton and the apostle Paul surfaced in a publishing meeting with Joey Paul and Byron Williamson of Integrity Publishers. Thank you, Joey and Bryon, for the belief you have had in this project. The fellowship we enjoy in publishing is a major blessing in my life.

Sealy Yates has been my literary agent for over twenty years. Sealy, you are the best at what you do, and you are constantly raising the bar for all of us who work with you! Thank you for your passionate commitment to the Captured by Grace campaign.

Cathy Lord took the responsibility of researching the life of John Newton, and I believe she may have read every book about him that has ever been published. Hardly a week went by that she did not drop something off at my desk that she had discovered about this remarkable man. In ways that only writers would understand, John Newton has become her personal friend. Thank you, Cathy, for the many hours you have invested in this book.

The most creative person I have ever met has an office just a few doors down from mine. Paul Joiner is just simply beyond description! Paul, it would be hard to point to any part of this project that you have not touched. You see everything in color! I wonder if your mind ever sleeps! I am so honored to have you as my friend and so blessed because of your imaginative input into all we do.

Rob Suggs has once again added his considerable gift to this project. Rob, your excellence in writing and editing is second to none. Thank you for making my writing assignments a high priority in your busy life.

Kevin Small has become an integral part of our publishing team. His understanding of marketing and distribution has dramatically changed the way we think about writing and publishing. Kevin, you stretch my mind and my faith, and I look forward to the times we spend together.

Because I pastor a large church and lead an international media ministry, writing can never be the first priority in my life. I write in the in-between hours of the day and night. I am able to do that because of the people of excellence God has placed around me. As my executive assistant at Turning Point Ministries, Diane Sutherland manages all my travel and my daily schedule. Diane, your commitment to details and your winsome, gracious personality make it possible for me to retreat from my busy world to study and write.

Barbara Boucher manages my office at Shadow Mountain and interacts daily with the many requests that come to my desk. Barbara, your heart for ministry is so evident. Thank you for your consistent and compassionate ministry.

My oldest son, David Michael Jeremiah, is a major player in just about everything I do. I love him deeply as my son, but I also respect him highly as a leader. He manages the priorities of a worldwide media ministry with an expertise beyond his years.

With the exception of my personal salvation, my wife Donna is the greatest blessing in my life. Without her encouragement, I would never have started to write. On those rare occasions when I have said I was never going to write another book, she has just looked at me and smiled. She knows me better than I know myself, and she loves me anyway!

Finally, I want to express my love and adoration to Almighty God who has given me His Son, filled me with His love, and captured me by His grace.

David Jeremiah
San Diego, January 2006

The Hunters *and* *the* Hunted

The hooded figure climbs quietly from his mount, praying that his arrival has gone undetected. He soothes his horse as he hitches her to a post, perhaps one hundred feet from his target. The moonlight dances on the hilt of his sword as he approaches the building and turns to wait for his companions.

There are five of them in all, armed and prepared for any resistance. The men cluster tightly behind an old wall to review the situation and their plan. The target is an old potter's shop, seldom used today. The heretics obviously believe they can perform their illicit worship rituals here with impunity. They are about to learn otherwise.

"Wait for my signal," whispers the leader. "I will pound forcefully upon the door once; and when you hear my fist, you shout for all your lungs are worth. If we create shock and fear, these idiots are all the easier to overpower. Draw your swords and clubs, and don't hesitate to strike if anyone puts up a fight. But most of them are probably women and children and elderly fools who will only whimper as we lead them away."

The five of them creep to the door and the windows of the old shed. The leader places his ear to the door and hears the quiet cadences of prayer. They will be on their knees with eyes shut—the most perfect time imaginable. He throws his fist against the wood, almost splintering it, and five deep voices begin to roar and threaten and terrorize.

As the soldiers hurtle through the doorway, they see the little band of worshipers for the first time. They're screaming in surprise and fear, of course. One infant begins to shriek. Several women begin to cry and cower, assuming the worst is in store for them. Five young men leap to their feet defensively. Yet the fools have brought no weapons at all. They had to know this was going to happen to them. The women restrain their men, who quickly realize the futility of striking back.

The chaos quickly fades to silence now, other than the sobbing of the inconsolable child. The soldiers bring their chains and begin clanging and shackling. One of the older women weeps quietly. Another does something very odd: she smiles at the leader. "I understand what you're doing," she says. "You're serving God to the best of your knowledge. If you could only see . . ."

"Shut up!" yells the leader, just managing to hold back his fist. "Don't patronize me with your imbecilic faith. I have mastered the Law of God, and there is nothing you can teach me. Save it for the rats who have the run of your prison cell." The woman looks at the floor, but there is no anger in her demeanor. Only a kind of resigned sadness.

The leader lingers behind as the Christians are led outside, from where they will be marched before the Council. He examines a crude wooden cross at the front of the room. What manner of insane cult would select such an article of worship? The heritage of faith is purity, holiness—what could be more impure and polluted than an instrument of Roman torture for the dregs of society?

Their founder, the Nazarene, fully deserved His cross. But the Pharisee wonders why these eccentrics risk the arrests and beatings they will now receive, on behalf of an odd rabbi who has been dead for some time now (whatever wild claims they may make about his tomb).

Then the Pharisee stops and listens very carefully to the quiet night. What was that scurrying sound outside? A footstep? The others have been gone for several minutes, and no one else is in this area. He has checked it carefully.

Saul feels the beginning of a chill along his spine. This has happened before—more than once. He roots out the Christians; he does his job; he is reminded of their strange calmness, their—what is the word for it? Some kind of irrational mercy. And always, as Saul is reflecting over the oddity of it all, he hears—the footsteps.

In those moments, he experiences a strange inside-out feeling that *he* is the one who is pursued, and that someone or something else is doing the pursuing. It's irrational, of course. What possible sense could it make? He is God's champion, defender of the faith. All he can do is soldier on, keep doing his job, root out these infidels, capture them one by one. Capture their faith, capture their—yes, that's the word—their *grace*.

The captain strolls along the Charles Towne battery, on the coast of Carolina. He gazes out to sea and listens to the cry of the gulls, wiping the perspiration from his brow. What humid lands, these colonies—a kingdom of mud and mosquitoes. Already he is feeling restless, impatient; if only he could busy himself with gathering the crew and loading the ship for the home voyage.

But there is business still to be done. That is the master purpose of every voyage, after all. One hundred sixty, perhaps one hundred seventy dollars per head. The final sum will be a comfortable one, providing that a good majority of the captives come ashore alive. On the last trip, nearly one-half of these Africans expired. There was hardly a profit to be made.

Yet the captain is not insensitive to such things. He would rather not be in attendance when the cargo hold is opened and the tally is taken. This is the distasteful cost of doing business; the cargo must be packed tightly. It must be chained and disciplined. Some of the natives will die of various diseases, from whippings, or from the heat. Some will even refuse to take bread. It is an unpleasant state of affairs, but England must have its commerce; the colonies must have their workers for crops of rice and indigo.

Yesterday, the captain witnessed an auction at the slave mart. He could not help but be disturbed by the cries of despair as children were parted from their mothers. After no more than a few minutes of this, he found he had to leave, to take a walk among the quieter streets. Let others keep the accounts and do the dickering.

As he strolls now by the seaside, he hears them again: footfalls directly behind him. The captain whirls quickly to find no intruder but the ocean wind. Once more, he reassures himself that his imagination is overactive. His restlessness must be to blame. He hasn't been sleeping well; there have been strange and unpleasant dreams.

And yet Captain Newton has felt it more and more on these business trips: a sense of being followed, of being watched. Even as he has pursued the fortune of slave trading, he has been unable to escape the feeling that it is *he* who is being pursued. Some steady footstep always out of eyesight, some whispered voice just beyond his hearing . . .

"Something relentless," John Newton mumbles to himself. "Something is pursuing us all."

PART ONE

GRACE
for the
PAST

CHAPTER ONE

The Captivating Presence *of* Grace

Amazing Grace, How Sweet the Sound

I t's autumn in New York. November 2004.
Freezing rain, weary drivers.
One carload of delinquents on a joyride.

Got the picture?

Their spree begins at the local cineplex. Bored with action flicks, the teenagers decide to act one out. They break into a car, grab a credit card, and proceed to a video store. There they charge four hundred dollars' worth of DVDs and video games.

Why not pick up a few groceries while they're at it? A surveillance tape catches the kids selecting a twenty-pound turkey.

Remember the turkey.

Pedal to the metal in a silver Nissan, the kids move along an irregular line intersecting with a Hyundai containing one Victoria Ruvolo. The two cars cross paths at approximately 12:30 a.m.

Victoria Ruvolo, forty-four, is heading for her Long Island home.

Having attended her fourteen-year-old niece's vocal recital, she looks forward to home and hearth—particularly hearth. She's ready to unravel the overcoat and scarves, burrow under an electric blanket, and rest her weary self.

Maybe the silver Nissan, approaching from the east, catches Victoria's eye—maybe not. Later, she won't be sure. She certainly won't recall the image of a teenage boy leaning out the window of the Nissan as the car approaches. Nor will she retain any memory of the bulky projectile taking flight from his hands.

This is the part about the turkey.

The twenty-pound bird crashes through Victoria's windshield. It bends the steering wheel inward, smashes into her face, and breaks every bone it encounters.

Victoria will remember none of this—frankly, a stroke of mercy. Eight hours of surgery and three weeks of recovery later, however, friends and family fill in the blanks. Victoria lies impassively in a bed in Stony Brook University Hospital and listens to every detail. Yet her emotions are difficult to discern, given the mask her face has become: shattered like pottery, now stapled together by titanium plates; an eye affixed by synthetic film; a wired jaw; a tracheotomy.

The public reaction is much more vigorous. The media has run with this story; weblogs follow every new detail of arrest and arraignment. Over Thanksgiving, New Yorkers whisper prayers of gratitude that they were not Victoria Ruvolo. Over Christmas, they cherish their health and their fortunes a little bit more than usual. Over the New Year, they cry out for justice.

Internet bloggers and TV pundits suggest what they'd do if they could be in a room for five minutes with those punks in the Nissan. They'd especially love to lay hands on Ryan Cushing, the eighteen-year-old who heaved the turkey. *His* face should be shattered. *His* life should lie in ruins. That's how the man in the street sees it.

But it's all in the hands of the justice system. On Monday, August 15, 2005, Ryan and Victoria meet face-to-restructured-face in the courtroom. Nine agonizing, titanium-bolted months have passed since the attack. Victoria manages to walk into the courtroom unaided, a victory in itself.

A trembling Ryan Cushing pleads guilty—to a lesser charge. Sentence: a trifling six months behind bars, five years probation, a bit of counseling, a dash of public service. People shake their heads in righteous indignation. Is that all the punishment we can dish out? When did this country become so soft on crime? Let's lock up all these criminals and throw away the key.

Who is responsible for this plea bargain anyway?

The victim. That's who. The victim requests leniency.

Ryan makes his plea and then turns to Victoria Ruvolo, all the essence of tough guy long since drained away. He is weeping with abandon. The attorney leads the assailant to the victim, and Victoria holds him tight, comforts him, strokes his hair, and offers reassuring words. "I forgive you," she whispers. "I want your life to be the best it can be." Tears mingle from mask of reconstruction and mask of remorse.

It takes quite an event to bring tears to the eyes of New York attorneys and magistrates. This is such an event. TV and radio reporters file their stories in voices that for once are hushed and respectful. The *New York Times* dubs it "a moment of grace."[1]

What do we do with such a story? It's beautiful, moving, inspiring—sure, all of those things. It's also *outrageous*. Why, it undermines every impulse of human nature, doesn't it? Let us be very honest. Would *you* have responded like Victoria Ruvolo? Surely you and I have been driven to a self-righteous frenzy over items far less dramatic. Some of us—some of the *best* of us—need one good incident on the expressway to bring out a snarl, a prolonged honking, a torrent of shouted invectives.

For that matter, remember when that fellow at work tried that little maneuver that really got your goat? You know the one—that petty little power play. How long did you seethe over that one? Or that woman at church who said that thing. Remember what she said and how you bristled? The look you gave her, and all that time you spent imagining what you'd like to say and do?

As for courtrooms, we've seen the opposite script play out. We've heard aggrieved families shouting at thugs as they stood to hear the verdict. And we've agreed with them, haven't we? It's just part of our constitution. Aren't we supposed to support justice and jeer at evil? Isn't it natural to affirm the process of punishing crime?

We're born that way. The smallest toddler retaliates to losing a toy to another child. She doesn't reclaim her toy calmly or dispassionately. She reacts in *outrage*. She seizes the plaything and shouts recriminations at its thief. It's all part of the human wiring. Work, church, playground—we're only human. We get mad *and* we get even.

Why, then, do we catch our breath upon observing behavior that precisely overturns these expectations?

Grace is shocking—something like the heavenly converse of a traffic accident. When love is returned for evil, we can't help stopping to rubberneck. Grace is the delivery of a jewel that nobody ordered, a burst of light in a room where everyone forgot it was dark.

Grace turns human politics on its head, right before our eyes. It renounces the entire conventional wisdom of social behavior. Grace suggests that human beings may be something more than honor graduates of the animal kingdom after all, that the rumors may be true that purity and goodness are real and alive.

Stories like that of Victoria Ruvolo transfix us for a moment. We find a smile, perhaps even shed a tear. It's like warming the soul at a hearth on a chilly night. Then it's right back to the struggle of the moment. We now resume our normal programming.

At least most of us do. Yet there are a rare few who find they cannot resume. The discovery of grace for them is like finding a knothole in the high gates of heaven. They cannot tear themselves away from peering into it. The light intoxicates their being. They wonder why, if this thing called grace is so magnificent—and if it is a standard option of every moment—why is it so rare and isolated? And urgently, pleadingly, the grace visionaries begin calling others to the knothole.

Such a man was the apostle Paul. He was once one of the seizers—the recriminators. These people, these Christians, had stolen his toy, and he was taking it back with a vengeance. They had laid hands on the faith of his fathers and polluted it. He would repay them with interest, galloping to far-flung regions just to torment them. That's when grace—or some Agent thereof—knocked him right out of the saddle, toppled his most precious assumptions, and took away his eyesight until he was ready to look hard at the thing he had refused to behold. And once his vision returned, that item was the only one he wished to see.

Paul changed his name and his person. He would write letter after letter to friends, to churches, to people he had never met—some who wouldn't be born for centuries. He spoke of many things in these letters, but he always came back around to the same theme: that moment of blinding grace on the Damascus Road, when sight came wrapped in blindness.

Our New Testament contains 155 references to grace; 130 of them come from the pen of Paul. The word opens, closes, and dominates every letter he wrote. It defines his teaching and his dearest hopes. Grace is the magnificent ideal by which he would measure his life and yours. The scourge of the martyrs has become the apostle of grace.

That's the startling power of one simple idea—the same power that transformed a ruthless slave trader to a timeless troubadour of liberation. John Newton shared Paul's obsession. In his elder years, he would sit by the fireplace in his former vicarage study at Olney. His once raging soul was now at peace. Just the same, he never wanted to forget the other John Newton—the one who traded in human cargo. Like Paul, his earthly eyesight was failing in latter years, but he could read the large letters he had painted on the wall over his fireplace:

Since thou wast precious in my sight,
thou has been honorable (Isaiah 43:4)
BUT
Thou shalt remember that thou wast a
bondman in the land of Egypt,
and the Lord thy God redeemed thee (Deuteronomy 15:15).

THE MELODY

It was John Newton's special joy as a pastor to craft sermons and hymns together. The Word and music were equally beloved to him, and he gave himself to both. For New Year's 1773, he turned his attention to 1 Chronicles 17:16–17: "Then King David went in and sat before the LORD; and he said: 'Who am I, O LORD God? And what is my house, that You have brought me this far? And yet this was a small thing in Your sight, O God; and You have also spoken of Your servant's house for a great while to come, and have regarded me according to the rank of a man of high degree, O LORD God.'"

The verses seemed to leap from the page before Newton's eye: *Who am I, Lord?* Why should King David, murderer and adulterer, receive the magnificent grace of God? Why should John Newton, trader of slaves? Such grace could only be described as amazing.

Yet the hymn that first emerged from Newton's pen might surprise the modern ear. For one thing, the melody was not the familiar one that has come down to the present day. It would be more than half a century before a man named William Walker would find just the right tune—a melody known as "New Britain." In Newton's time, as many as twenty different melodies might be used interchangeably. Even that immortal title had yet to assert itself. The hymn's original title? "Faith's Review and Expectation"—not exactly catchy enough for the pop charts, then or now.

There were more verses than we often recognize too. Many people claim to know all the verses of "Amazing Grace" by heart, but can they sing the lines below? These originally followed the present third verse:

> *The Lord has promised good to me,*
> *His word my hope secures;*
> *He will my shield and portion be,*
> *As long as life endures.*

> *Yes, when this flesh and heart shall fail,*
> *And mortal life shall cease,*
> *I shall possess, within the veil,*
> *A life of joy and peace.*

> *The earth shall soon dissolve like snow,*
> *The sun forbear to shine;*
> *But God, who call'd me here below,*
> *Will be forever mine.*

But a verse is missing, isn't it? The one that may be your favorite. What about "When we've been there ten thousand years"? The closing stanza you and I know and love first appeared in 1909. Edwin

Othello Excell, himself a prolific composer, inserted the final piece in the puzzle, completing the standard version of the hymn. Excell replaced verses four, five, and six with four lines that John Newton never wrote. How did it happen?

In the year 1852, antislavery sentiment had come to a boil in America. Newton would have heartily approved. Harriet Beecher Stowe's novel *Uncle Tom's Cabin* appeared that year, including a version of "Amazing Grace" that added these lines:

> *When we've been there ten thousand years*
> *Bright shining as the sun,*
> *We've no less days to sing God's praise,*
> *Than when we first begun.*

Excell admired this version excerpt with its vision set in eternal glory. He grafted these new lines to the existing ones, and we've sung it that way ever since.

The English used the song on occasion. Across the sea in South Carolina, the hymn was first published with a melody. That hymnal, *The Southern Harmony*, sold an amazing six hundred thousand copies in 1850—two years before Excell added his "ten thousand."

Years came and passed, and so did new hymnals and musical fashions. "Amazing Grace" was one nice hymn among many until, of all things, the age of acid rock.

In 1970, when electric guitars and angry lyrics ruled the charts, folk singer Judy Collins released an audacious track: an a capella rendition of the old hymn "Amazing Grace." Without the drums, without the backbeat, the result was a revelation to young ears. By early 1971, the song was a hit in England and America. Finally, three recorded minutes that the elderly and their flower-child grandkids could listen to together.

Then in 2004, Bill Moyers produced an entire documentary about the song for public television. He paid tribute to the mysterious power of a simple hymn that had traveled so far with so many adventures. Judy Collins, reprising her hit, told of its support during her bout with alcoholism. Opera singer Jessye Norman rendered a concert version. Country singer Johnny Cash used it to connect with imprisoned criminals. The song cast its spell in many worlds, whether sung by the Boys Choir of Harlem, shaped-note choruses in the Appalachian foothills, or among Japanese worshipers.

The hymn is heard at Olympic ceremonies and presidential inaugurations. It is considered essential in a time of disaster; a crisis such as the one of September 11, 2001; or at any moment of somber mood. It has become a de facto national anthem for events of magnitude.

Shoppers at Amazon.com may choose from among 3,832 separate recordings of John Newton's old hymn. It comes in every style, crosses every line, and reaches any and every ear. And when it is announced in a church service, people stand a little taller to sing it. They lift their voices a bit higher. Some of them feel that, just for a moment, they are catching a glimpse through the gates of heaven.

THE MAN

St. Augustine wrapped a powerful thought in vivid imagery when he said, "God always pours His grace into empty hands." The hands of John Newton could not have been emptier.

His father commanded a merchant ship and was always at sea. His mother raised him the best she could, schooling him in Scripture and sacred song. Mother and son attended a chapel near the Tower of London. In a nation in which 99 percent of the people were affiliated with the Church of England, Elizabeth Newton insisted upon an independent congregation.[2]

Just before his seventh birthday, John Newton lost his mother. It didn't take the old captain long to remarry and dispatch the boy to a boarding school. His was a childhood out of a Dickens novel. Unwanted children were often abandoned and abused at such schools. John left school and returned home. The elder Newton shrugged, put his young son on a ship, and began taking him along on his travels.

By the age of seventeen, John Newton's world was the open sea. The world of the Spirit, as lovingly taught by his mother, had vanished over his horizon. For seven years he declined into rebellion. Like some today, he mixed and matched convenient ideas to create his own religion, making "a shipwreck of faith, hope and conscience." In his own words, his "delight and habitual practice was wickedness," and he "neither feared God nor regarded men." In short, he was "a slave to doing wickedness and delighted in sinfulness."[3]

After a short stint in the wartime navy, Newton decided the regimented military life was not for him. He left in search of his father in the belief that his father could secure his release. It proved a futile move, as the deserter was quickly captured. He took a public beating, was stripped of his rank as midshipman, and was placed in shackles. Finally he managed to get on an Africa-bound freighter. There, in the shadow of the Dark Continent, John Newton sought to be lost where he could not be found. He could abandon himself to a life of dissolution.

Newton took up with a Portuguese slave trader on the island of Plantain, just off Sierra Leone on the western coast. The man's African wife was hostile to her husband's new friend and forced him to eat scraps from her plate like a dog. His life and fortunes had reached low ebb. Perhaps he remembered a story his mother once read him—something about another rebellious son far from home, eating among the pigs.

Finally, John Newton was taken aboard a slave ship, where he was quartered with the captain. Then, in March 1748, somewhere in the North Atlantic, grace arrived. The hand of God rescued a shipwrecked soul. If it could happen to Paul on the road to Damascus, it could come to Newton on the voyage to Britannia. In chapter 6, we'll hear more of his conversion story.

Two years later, Newton was married. But just as the storm seemed over, he began to be troubled by fits and seizures that precluded a life at sea. So he stayed home and worked as a tide surveyor at the docks of Liverpool. With plenty of time on his hands, he began to fill in the great gaps of a childhood that provided little formal education. He studied Greek, Hebrew, and Syriac. He read classic theological works in Latin, English, and French. More and more, he found himself drawn to that old book that brought memories of his mother—the Christian Scriptures.

Then the people wanted a pastor. In 1754, he accepted a calling in Olney, where he would serve for sixteen years. At the next church, this time in London, he served God and men for twenty-eight years. An aging but contented man, at the age of seventy-two he marveled that "such a wretch should not only be spared and pardoned, but reserved to the honor of preaching the gospel, which he blasphemed and renounced."[4] He preached the Gospel until the venerable age of eighty-one.

The melody, however, lingers on.

THE MESSAGE

Man and melody—each sailed quite a journey. Newton's hymn, of course, has easily outlived him. People wonder at the power of "Amazing Grace." What is so amazing about it? Like so many things, it defies the dissection we might give a frog in science class. We can't quite discover the secret, for the notes are the same as those on any piano. The words are transcendent, but no more so than the stanzas of any number of other hymns—"Holy, Holy, Holy," for example. No public relations firm has accounted for its influence. No pope or prelate has sanctified it. But there it is, a cherished piece of our lives.

Some have attempted to bottle its inspiration, filter its doctrine, and reduce it to an anthem of generic wellness. "Amazing Grace," to some, is simply "a greater sense of consciousness" or "the power of human potential," a "moment of intense awareness" or "experiencing the interconnectedness of all things." It is "being aware of the unity of which we are all a part" or "the unseen forces that are all around us." It is "relinquishing the ego," "achieving mental clarity," or "finding spiritual illumination."

For M. Scott Peck it is "hidden in the 95 percent of our consciousness of which we are unaware."[5] For Judy Collins, it is "letting go, bottoming out, seeing the light, turning it over, trusting the universe, breathing in, breathing out, going with the flow."[6] For folk singer Joan Baez, "it's a state I would like to be in for more than thirty seconds a day."[7] For Pete Seeger, "Grace means harmony . . . the law of gravity throughout the universe a kind of harmony . . . or the way that mathematics works."[8]

We can only imagine what John Newton would make of all this—perhaps express bewilderment over such nebulous metaphysical puffery. He would point out that his verses do no more, and no less, than tell the old, old story—the one that never grows old. They tell of the loving Father and the lost son. They speak of the incredible joy of salvation from the clutches of sin, of the amazingness of grace.

Perhaps it is not the song after all; perhaps it has never been the song but the idea—and the fact that this hymn is simply the one that best captures the lightning.

The lightning is grace. As Martyn Lloyd-Jones has written: "There is no more wonderful word than 'grace.' It means unmerited favor or kindness shown to one who is utterly undeserving. . . . It is not merely a free gift, but a free gift to those who deserve the exact opposite, and it is given to us while we are 'without hope and without God in the world.' "⁹

Someone has written that *grace* is a five-letter word that is often spelled J-E-S-U-S. For, if Newton's hymn was the melody that embodied the idea, Jesus was the Man. He was the once-and-for-all, perfect human image of grace, of love, of truth. "In the beginning was the Word, and the Word was with God, and the Word was God. . . . And the Word became flesh and dwelt among us, and we beheld His glory, the glory as of the only begotten of the Father, full of grace and truth. . . . For the law was given through Moses, but grace and truth came through Jesus Christ" (John 1:1, 14, 17).

In the Greek tongue of Paul's day, the word for "grace" was *charis*. It carried the connotation of graciousness or favor. But the term evolved in the Greek world until it meant the actual gift, the concrete expression of kindness. Grace happens. As Paul explained it, "The free gift is not like the offense. For if by the one man's offense many died, much more the grace of God and the gift by the grace of the one Man, Jesus Christ, abounded to many" (Romans 5:15).

Grace happens, and it acts. "For by grace you have been saved through faith, and that not of yourselves, it is the gift of God" (Ephesians 2:8).

Such grace can come only from God. It is the gift unsought, unmerited, unlimited. For no matter what we have done, no matter the depth of our transgression, the darkness of our hearts—grace overrules them all. God pursues us relentlessly, He will not give us up, and once He has captured us, He won't let us go.

These are the broad outlines of the great idea. Yet it is as if we are mapping an uncharted territory—surveying the bounds of heaven, if you will. We can never take in the whole expanse. Grace is too dazzling, too bright, for it is powered by the holy heart of God. Trying to comprehend it in whole is like staring directly into one thousand suns.

Grace is as infinite and transcendent as the God from whom it flows. He is "the God of all grace" (1 Peter 5:10), and He is abounding with mercy for the merciless, help for the helpless, redemption for anyone and everyone. There is no limit to the throng of guests invited to dine at the Master's overflowing table.

As Griffith Thomas has said, "All this in full measure and overflowing abundance, because of nothing in the object, and because of everything in the Giver, God himself."[10]

Grace is the bridge over a chasm that seemed infinite—the canyon between our depravity and His holiness. That bridge is wide and sturdy and sure, beckoning to us to cross over into a life too wonderful for us to imagine.

THE MERCY

At the heart of the mystery is an essential concept: the idea of mercy. We must understand grace, at least within the limits of our comprehension; we must understand mercy. And we must be clear on how the two ideas intersect.

We often use the words as if they are synonyms—one and the same. In fact, there are passages in the New Testament that make that appear to be so. A few scholars have put forward the neat and simple proposition that the Old Testament uses *mercy* while the New Testament speaks of *grace*.

The truth is more elusive, like the words themselves. Think of it this way: Mercy is God withholding the punishment we rightfully deserve. Grace is God not only withholding that punishment but offering the most precious of gifts instead.

Mercy withholds the knife from the heart of Isaac.
Grace provides a ram in the thicket.

Mercy runs to forgive the Prodigal Son.
Grace throws a party with every extravagance.

Mercy bandages the wounds of the man beaten by the robbers.
Grace covers the cost of his full recovery.

Mercy hears the cry of the thief on the cross.
Grace promises paradise that very day.

Mercy pays the penalty for our sin at the cross.
Grace substitutes the righteousness of Christ for our wickedness.

Mercy converts Paul on the road to Damascus.
Grace calls him to be an apostle.

Mercy saves John Newton from a life of rebellion and sin.
Grace makes him a pastor and author of a timeless hymn.

Mercy closes the door to hell.
Grace opens the door to heaven.

Mercy withholds what we have earned.
Grace provides blessings we have not earned.

In Victor Hugo's *Les Misérables,* Jean Valjean is a guileless, unassuming man until he is imprisoned during the French Revolution for stealing a loaf of bread in order to feed his starving family. After completing nineteen years of hard labor, he is bitter and angry toward both society and God.

Monseigneur Myriel, a seventy-four-year-old bishop in southeastern France, has also suffered greatly during the Revolution. All that remains of the bishop's aristocratic heritage are six knives and forks, a soup ladle, and two candlesticks. His experience has taught the bishop compassion for the indigent, and he ministers to them as a humble servant.

After four days of freedom, with repeated denials of food or shelter, the weary and hungry Valjean becomes a desperate man. He arrives at the door of the bishop's home. The hardened Valjean, mistaking it for an inn, brashly storms into the kitchen where he is confounded by the warm welcome he receives from the bishop. That night, while the household is asleep, Valjean leaves the first mattress and white sheets he has known in nineteen years and stealthily fills a knapsack with the bishop's treasured silverware and disappears into the darkness.

In the morning, the bishop corroborates the shackled Valjean's claim to the gendarmes that the silver has been given to him. The bishop asks them to release Valjean and says to him, "I'm glad to see you. But I gave you the candlesticks, too, which are silver like the rest and for which you can certainly get two hundred francs. Why did you not carry them away with your forks and spoons?"

Incredulously, Valjean asks the bishop, "Is it true that I am to be released?"

The bishop assures him that he is free and adds, "My friend, before you go, here are your candlesticks. Take them." Then he adds, "Do not forget, never forget, that you have promised to use this money in becoming an honest man. . . . Jean Valjean, my brother, you no longer belong to evil, but to good. It is your soul that I am buying for you. I withdraw it from [heinous] thoughts and from the spirit of perdition, and I give it to God."

Troubled by the grace offered to him, Valjean visualizes the contrast of the darkness in his own soul with the harsh light of love that has penetrated his bitterness. "A gentle light rested over this life and this soul. It seemed to him that he beheld Satan by the light of Paradise." It was certain indeed, "he was no longer the same man, that everything about him was changed." The bishop had "filled the whole soul of this wretched man with a magnificent radiance."

Twenty-four hours after his theft, Valjean returns to the scene of his crime and is observed "in the attitude of prayer, kneeling on the pavement in the shadow in front of the door of the gentle bishop.

A moment of grace can change a lifetime. In fact, a moment of grace can change an eternity.

Moments *of* Grace

If you're suffering from guilt or a slip-sliding self-image, skim back over chapter 1 and underline the phrases that most impress you, like: *I forgive you . . . God always pours His grace into empty hands . . . Unmerited favor . . . Unlimited . . . Grace is a five-letter word spelled J-E-S-U-S . . . Grace is a bridge over a chasm that seemed infinite . . .* Then choose one particular underlined statement and turn it into a prayer, asking God to make you a recipient of His amazing grace and a conveyer of it to others.

Ask yourself, "How can I be more like Victoria Ruvolo, who forgave her assailant and wanted his life to be the best it could be?" Is there someone you can forgive today? And as you close this chapter, don't forget to sing! Every time you close this book, walk away with a few bars of "Amazing Grace" playing in your mind or floating from your lips.

CHAPTER TWO

The Compassionate Plan *of* Grace

That Saved a Wretch Like Me

W
hen was the last time you met a wretch strolling down the avenue? How about a transgressor? A miscreant? A worker of iniquity?

Look those words up in a dusty old dictionary, and you'll find an entire arsenal of powerful words for sin and its perpetrators. Yet many of these words are on the endangered vocabulary list today. They grow musty and unfamiliar from lack of use.

The question is, in a world such as ours, why would so many colorful and descriptive terms for wickedness go out of style? Sin is still in; only the names have changed. Debauchers have been replaced by "compulsive personality types." We don't hear much about iniquity, but we do make plenty of references to "unproductive personal habits." Nobody this side of the Grimm Brothers is actually *wicked* today—just a lot of folks with "behavioral disorders," right? If anyone in our society does something socially unacceptable, just blame the chemistry and find the right prescription drug. If we can't eliminate sin in practice, we'll change its name and talk around it until nobody recognizes the problem.

A few years ago, the *Wall Street Journal* placed an advertisement in the *New York Times* observing that our generation has dismantled its old, sturdy frames of reference for personal behavior. The idea of guilt was swept away, leaving people to make their own judgment calls on moral issues. The ad concluded that "many wrecked people could have used a road map."[1]

Jettisoning the guilt trip sounds like a lot of fun at first—a real party. Only later, when it is too late, do we wander through the moral debris and wonder if our freedom was truly free. That's when the old terminology seems so much more descriptive—words such as *wickedness* and *wretch*. Throw in *remorse* and *penitence*.

We find the word *wretch*, of course, in "Amazing Grace." Let me ask you, how do you feel when you sing that phrase "a wretch like me"? Some of us belt out that line with a huge smile, as if we had no clue what we were proclaiming about ourselves! Others pay more attention, and they don't like that phrase one bit. Who is this songbook calling a wretch? There have been attempts to remove the W word from the standard hymnal.

Wretch. The term is often confused with *retch*, which is not even its distant cousin. At the risk of indelicacy, we'll simply point out that the one without the *w* descends from a Middle English term meaning to clear one's throat. *Wretch*, on the other hand, descends from a more ancient lineage—it comes from an Old English term meaning someone who is miserable, an exile. That's illuminating, for what are exiles but what the *Wall Street Journal* called "wrecked people who need a road map"?

A wretch is one miserable human being in a self-imposed exile.

Like the Prodigal Son. Like John Newton. As a matter of fact, your dictionary should carry a head shot of John Newton with its listing for *wretch*. Let's get back to his story.

A Wretched Exile

To understand the wonder of grace through the eyes of Newton, you must have some idea of the wretchedness of his exile.

We rejoin Newton as a young man on the deck of one of his first sailing vessels. He is depressed, but Prozac won't be invented for centuries. He is raging, but there are no handy anger-management books around. Therefore he sits beneath the moon, stares into the restless sea, and weighs two options:

a) Maybe he will commit suicide;
b) Maybe he will murder the captain.

Perhaps by the restraining hand of God, he chooses

c) None of the above.

Newton wrote a letter in 1754 saying that before he had reached the age of twenty, he was never an hour in anyone's company without attempting to corrupt their character. He once said of himself, "My daily life was a course of the most terrible blasphemy and profaneness. I don't believe that I have ever since met so daring a blasphemer as myself. Not content with common profanities and cursing, I daily invented new ones . . ."[2]

His soul was deep in exile, farther away than any ship could have carried him.

In his book *Not the Way It's Supposed to Be: A Breviary of Sin,* theologian Cornelius Plantinga Jr. assures us that we can never arrive at any definition of *grace* without sin as our point of departure. Cheap grace, he says, trivializes the cross of Christ. How can we avert our eyes from a cross that is drenched in holy blood? It was for sin that God, clothed in flesh, writhed in agony on our behalf. It was for iniquity; for wickedness; for every manner of wretched, despicable evil that He submitted to beating and humiliation and finally the obscenity of death itself.

Grace can only shine in its ultimate brilliance because it emerges from ultimate darkness. Therefore, Plantinga points out, we load up on bland and inoffensive modern worship practices, "seeker-sensitive" though they may be, at our own peril. Catchy praise choruses and positive-thinking sermons are crowd pleasers, but sometimes the praise bands drown out the sobering reality of sin—not "unproductive habits," but *sin*—and the consequent demand for confession, repentance, and forgiveness.[3]

This is not to weigh in on all the issues that surround our modern worship but to question any gathering of the saints where sin is swept under the sanctuary carpet. That could happen against the background of a pipe organ or an electric guitar. The point is that we must confront the true enemy in clear terms.

Paul was the apostle of grace, but he never denied the apostasy of sin. In fact, it was his very honesty on that subject that caught John Newton's despairing eye. The exile was intrigued that a man like Paul could call himself the "chief" of sinners (1 Timothy 1:15), that God would pluck His champion from the roster of the enemy.

Newton read Paul's words in 1 Timothy 1:13–14 over and over: "I was formerly a blasphemer, a persecutor, and an insolent man; but I obtained mercy because I did it ignorantly in unbelief. And the grace of our Lord was exceedingly abundant, with faith and love which are in Christ Jesus."

Abundant grace for abundant sin. John Newton couldn't stop thinking about the implications of such an idea.

PRELUDE TO GRACE

Paul was not one to airbrush the scandal of his own past. His résumé, as it crops up in his writings, always includes the hard truth that he was the "least of the apostles," in his words, because he had the blood of the martyrs on his hands (1 Corinthians 15:9). He was "less than the least of all the saints" (Ephesians 3:8). He was the "chief" of sinners (1 Timothy 1:15).

But the truth of it, as Paul shows in Romans 3, is that none of us has clean hands. The apostle goes to the Old Testament to make his case—Ecclesiastes, five psalms, one citation from Isaiah. Five times he uses the words *none* or *all,* for none are righteous; all are ruined and helpless in the sight of God. We are a world of exiles. As it is written:

> *"There is none righteous, no, not one;*
> *There is none who understands;*
> *There is none who seeks after God.*
> *They have all turned aside;*
> *They have together become unprofitable;*
> *There is none who does good, no, not one."*
> *"Their throat is an open tomb;*
> *With their tongues they have practiced deceit;"*
> *"The poison of asps is under their lips;"*
> *"Whose mouth is full of cursing and bitterness."*
> *"Their feet are swift to shed blood;*
> *Destruction and misery are in their ways;*
> *And the way of peace they have not known."*
> *"There is no fear of God before their eyes." (Romans 3:10–18)*

The chorus to Paul's sorrowful song is "no one—not even one." He comes around to that refrain five times. Lest we cling to any shred of self-righteousness, Paul tells us again and again.

This is a message no one wants to hear, for the upshot of it is that you can be the most upright citizen of your town, and still, before the revealing light of heaven, you are a miserable wretch at the mercy of a holy God. You can have a crime-free record, perfect standing with the IRS, the works of Mother Teresa, the passion of Paul, and the conviction of Gandhi, and you still stand accused and convicted before the perfect standards of an infinitely righteous Judge.

Here are more words we'd rather not sing about ourselves: *total depravity.* We would prefer to reserve such a term for child abusers, pornographers, and terrorists. But Paul shakes his head sadly and says none of us is righteous. No, not one.

Our depravity doesn't come in half-doses: *total* means just that. Charles Swindoll has written that if depravity were blue, we'd be blue all over. We'd bleed blue, think blue thoughts, and have no possibility of a single fragment of a second when our heart, soul, and mind weren't flooded in blue. You could be as colorful a personality as you wish, but every tint of the rainbow would be overwhelmed by blue.[4]

Ivan Turgenev, the nineteenth-century Russian novelist and playwright, said, "I don't know what the heart of a bad man is like, but I do know what the heart of a good man is like and it is terrible."

And Aleksandr Solzhenitsyn writes, "If only there were evil people somewhere insidiously committing evil deeds; and it were necessary only to separate them from the rest of us and destroy them. But the line dividing good and evil cuts through the heart of every human being. And who is willing to destroy a piece of his own heart?"[6] Sin cuts its merciless swath through the entire human race, not missing a single heart.

On the other hand, there *is* some good news. Very significant good news! Total depravity meets its match in total grace; one infinite value cancels out another.

In the end, we must acknowledge the darkness within us and the light that comes only from God. Both are unrelenting, and both define every moment of our life. Every atom in our bodies is infected by the disease of sin, but every atom may likewise be covered by the grace of God. The vilest offender can reap the deepest joys of heaven.

The only requirement comes in two supreme realizations: first, that we are totally contaminated; second, that we are totally forgiven only through the love and grace and sacrifice of our Lord Jesus Christ.

Paul has shown us the first of those realities. Now, with great joy, he turns his attention to the second.

PRINCIPLES OF GRACE

Get ready, for we will look now at five of the most important verses in the Bible. This section of Romans may be possibly the most important single paragraph ever written.

John Bunyan, author of *Pilgrim's Progress*, attributed his conversion to these verses. Bible scholar Donald Grey Barnhouse drew a great heart across them in his Bible. He declared that they constitute the heart of Romans, the heart of the New Testament, the heart of the Word of God itself. Imagine: the whole galaxy of revelation from our Father revolving around this single point, the ground zero of our spiritual universe.[7]

Now as we stand upon this holy ground, Paul shows us seven components of the grace of God. Talk about your vocabulary! These words will never grow musty in the dictionary of heaven. They are words such as *grace, faith, justification, redemption, freely*—the antidote for *wretch, iniquity, depravity,* and the rest. Learn these verses, know the meanings of these words, and you have passed a master's course in salvation science.

Paul wrote this textbook of grace through the inspiration of the Holy Spirit. John Newton escaped his exile here. John Bunyan made his pilgrimage in this passage. This little site in your Bible is the missing link between life and death, flesh and spirit, creature and Creator. And every one of us must pass this spring and drink deeply if we are to understand who we are and how we may be rescued from ourselves.

Grace: Apart from Works

> *But now the righteousness of God apart from the law is revealed.*
> —ROMANS 3:21

In the entire world, only two religions may be found. The first of them might be called the religion of divine accomplishment. The second is the religion of human achievement. Paul sets these two conflicting ideas against one another.

The apostle knows from firsthand experience that human achievement is designed for failure. He has lived it both ways and found human achievement to be a dead end. He once surpassed every standard of excellence established for a Hebrew Pharisee, and it all came to nothing. And he will tell us over and over, in each of his epistles, that works can never suffice. We might as well try building a ladder to heaven.

> But to him who does not work but believes on Him who
> justifies the ungodly, his faith is accounted for righteousness.
> (Romans 4:5)

For by grace you have been saved through faith, and that not of yourselves; it is the gift of God, not of works, lest anyone should boast. (Ephesians 2:8–9)

[God] has saved us and called us with a holy calling, not according to our works, but according to His own purpose and grace which was given to us in Christ Jesus before time began. (2 Timothy 1:9)

Not by works of righteousness which we have done, but according to His mercy He saved us, through the washing of regeneration and renewing of the Holy Spirit. (Titus 3:5)

Knowing that a man is not justified by the works of the law but by faith in Jesus Christ. . . . I do not set aside the grace of God; for if righteousness comes through the law, then Christ died in vain. (Galatians 2:16, 21)

Grace: Accepted by Faith

Even the righteousness of God, through faith in Jesus Christ.
—ROMANS 3:22

Now we turn to the idea of faith. Listen to the frequency with which it comes through Paul's pen in Romans 3:

"God set forth as a propitiation by His blood, through faith" (v. 25).
"The justifier of the one who has faith in Jesus" (v. 26).
"A man is justified by faith" (v. 28).
"Justify the circumcised by faith" (v. 30).
"And the uncircumcised through faith" (v. 30).
"Do we then make void the law through faith?" (v. 31).

As noted British pastor Charles Spurgeon once said, faith is believing Christ is who He said He was and that He'll do what He promised to do—and then living accordingly. That way our faith is "accounted for righteousness" (Romans 4:5). And we have "peace with God through our Lord Jesus Christ" (Romans 5:1).

God's grace meets human faith, and peace is declared in the war between heaven and earth.

Grace: Available to All Who Believe

> *. . . to all and on all who believe. For there is no difference;*
> *for all have sinned and fall short of the glory of God.*
> —ROMANS 3:22–23

Key word: *all.* That is one immense three-letter word, for it measures the width of God's grace and the height of His love. God's net is as large as the number of people who are willing to fall into its safety. No one is outside the scope of His grace. There are no distinctions within the nation of the sinful, no pecking order within the league of the elect.

There are indeed degrees of sin. A jaywalker receives a lighter sentence than a murderer. But all of that is earthly reckoning—nit-picking by the standard of heaven. Because a millionth of a molecule of sin contaminates a soul, *all* are found guilty. And because grace cleanses us from sin just as absolutely, we find ourselves standing at the throne of grace without any human ranks or measurements. All are equally pure and clean before God. You and the apostle Paul will stand together, equally righteous in God's sight. The Father will look upon each of you and see only the purity of His own Son.

Grace: Attained by Justification

Being justified . . .
—ROMANS 3:24

At the center point of this centerpiece passage we find the concept of justification. Don't be fooled—the idea is more complex than you may suppose. I may forgive you for doing me some wrong, but I haven't justified you. The judge may throw your case out of court, but it doesn't affect your true guilt or innocence. Pardon simply takes away the punishment for a sin. Justification erases any record of your transgression.

Jesus infuriated the religious leaders by this very act. He forgave sins of which He was not even the victim! How could He, as a third party, forgive one person's transgression against another?

He can do so because He is God, because He is pure, and because He chooses to be a third party to every wrong act we can ever commit. Christ removes not only the penalty for our sin; He cleanses us completely from its slightest taint. You and I stand before God as if we lived a life of utter purity and perfection.

Forgiveness says, "I'm going to let you slide this time." Justification says, "I'm going to remove the offense from all memory, as if it never occurred." It forgives and forgets. The president can pardon, but he cannot reinstate the criminal to the position of one who has not broken the law. God does both—that's the key to justification.

John Stott writes that "justification is not a synonym for amnesty . . . [but] an act of justice, of gracious justice. . . . When God justifies sinners, he is not declaring bad people to be good, or saying that they are not sinners after all; he is pronouncing them legally righteous, free from any liability to the broken law, because he himself in his Son has borne the penalty of their law-breaking."[8]

Grace: Awarded Freely

Being justified freely . . .
—ROMANS 3:24

You already know the Latin word for "freely": *gratis*. Revelation 22:17 tells us that the water of life is *gratis* to anyone who wants it. Jesus says in Matthew 10:8 that *gratis* we have received, and *gratis* we should give.

A beggar presses his nose against a plate-glass window. The smells of the restaurant are intoxicating to him. He has no work, no shelter, and no hope. His stomach growls in protest as he watches the well-dressed, well-fed patrons enjoy their steak and lobster dinners. This is the finest restaurant in town. Who is he kidding by even looking upon the elegance of their feast? As a matter of fact, here comes the waiter to shoo him away, unappetizing scenery that he has become.

But the waiter's face bears no rebuke. Instead, compassion is written across it. "I've brought you our finest entrée," says the waiter, uncovering a sumptuous plate. The vagrant's eyes grow wide, and he reaches for the embarrassing pocket change that is all he can offer. "Put your coins away," laughs the waiter. "This one's on our owner, who spotted you from the window. He knows you could never afford such a meal, and he offers this one *freely*. Come back again when you're hungry."

You are an invited guest at the heavenly banquet, not a paying customer. *Gratis*—you have to like that word.

Grace: Acquired Through Redemption

Being justified freely by His grace through the redemption that is in Christ Jesus.
—ROMANS 3:24

Have you ever redeemed a coupon? Sure enough, we've come to the language of the marketplace.

Paul had walked through the streets of Rome and Corinth, where slaves were bought and sold like apples from a fruit stand. He knew that we are all slaves to sin and guilt, more helpless and humbled than the most shackled slave. Jesus steps into the street, produces payment, and sets us free.

But that illustration is lacking to say the least. In reality, Jesus used no coin but the precious exchange of His blood. It's not the same as a rich man reaching into his wallet for a few dollars when he has millions. Jesus puts up all that He has. He buys our liberation through His own suffering. He becomes the slave so that the real slave may go free.

That is why Christ is our *Redeemer*. Princeton theologian Benjamin Warfield loved applying that title to his Lord, because it reminds us not only of our precious gift but its ultimate price: "Whenever we pronounce it, the cross is placarded before our eyes and our hearts are filled with loving remembrance not only that Christ has given us salvation, but that he paid a mighty price for it."[9]

Grace: Accomplished Through Propitiation

Whom God set forth as a propitiation by His blood . . .
—ROMANS 3:25

Yet another beautiful word sadly lacking in current parlance is *propitiation.* It is one of the most powerful and profound terms in the biblical vocabulary. Yet it is used sparingly in the sacred Word of God. A mere four times we come across it in the New Testament. On each occasion, it provides a glimpse of our salvation through the eyes of God himself.

Its Old Testament usage provides a few clues to the mystery of propitiation. The ark of the covenant was a gold-covered wooden box about one yard long. The treasure it held was no less than the stone tablets of the Law, etched by the finger of God and borne from Mount Sinai in the hands of Moses. The box had a cover known as the mercy seat, which held two cherubim that faced one another from each end. The wings of these cherubim stretched upward then forward, nearly meeting in the middle over the ark.

The symbolism of the wings told everyone that God dwelled above the ark. Yet the ark provided a picture of judgment—a feeling of dread. For, as James Montgomery Boice points out, God looked down from heaven between the wings of those cherubim and saw the ark's cargo of commandments. They were as surely and injudiciously broken as the tablets themselves, which Moses had hurled in frustration. Disobedience called for judgment.

Ah, but there is that covering. What is it called? The *mercy* seat.

You see, once a year, on the Day of Atonement, the Jewish high priest entered the holy of holies to make atonement for the people's sins. He entered to make *propitiation*—the very word that comes down to us from Hebrew to Greek, translated as "mercy seat." The priest sprinkled the blood of an animal sacrifice upon the mercy seat.

This changed things. Now, as God looked down, He didn't immediately see those broken laws on shattered tablets. Instead He saw the blood of innocence, a humble offering of repentance. And forgiveness became possible—through propitiation.

How many herds of rams would it take to cover all our sins? How often must this ritual be repeated? The final answer, of course, was the blood of God's own Son.[10]

John writes, "He Himself is the propitiation for our sins, and not for ours only but also for the whole world" (1 John 2:2). There is enough room beneath those angels' wings for every one of us.

THE FOUNTAIN OF GRACE

In the dark background of John Newton's life, we come across a man by the name of William Cowper (pronounced *Cooper*).

Born in 1731, Cowper shared something in common with Newton. His mother died when he was small. And he, too, was abruptly shipped away to a boarding school. Cowper, small and shy, became the target of bullies and persecution. All the love and security of his life seemed to have been replaced by abandonment and victimization.

As Cowper grew, his studies became his refuge; he particularly enjoyed poetry and literature. His mother had been a Donne, coming from the family of the Christian poet John Donne, who wrote, "No man is an island." But his mother was dead, and Cowper felt very much like an island.

His father insisted that young William enter the legal field. When it came time for his final examination, the student suffered an emotional breakdown and attempted suicide. After this, he couldn't regain any emotional equilibrium. "I was a stricken deer that left the herd," he writes.[11]

By now, Cowper had decided that all life and all its agents were aligned against him; he had been born under a curse. He threw away his Bible in scorn, saying that God was one more bully out to get him. As a matter of fact, so was everyone else, for Cowper suffered from acute paranoia. The world was one great conspiracy against him. He had become a wretched exile with no road map home.

After his failed suicide attempt, Cowper was diagnosed with *hypochondrial melancholy*. That's when some of his few friends recommended a mental asylum. The grace of God here enters the story.

Dr. Nathaniel Cotton, poet and Christian, happened to be the physician in charge. For eighteen months, Cowper showed positive progress. Dr. Cotton helped Cowper recover his love for poetry and the written word. He patiently explained the infinite magnitude of God's grace, which was great enough to cover all His children, even William Cowper. Could it be that instead of all things being in league against him, all things worked for the good of those who loved this God? The patient listened, and he tried to believe. One day he succeeded.

Cowper picked up a Bible and read Romans 3, the heart of the Gospel. As it happened one day for Luther, for Wesley, for Newton, and for every desperate soul whose heart has ever despaired itself into the arms of God—Cowper succumbed to the holy pursuit of the Lord. The power of propitiation made it all come to life for him.

Later he would write, "Immediately I received strength to believe it, and the full beams of the Sun of Righteousness shone upon me. I saw the sufficiency of the atonement He had made, my pardon sealed in His blood, and all the fullness and completeness of His justification. In a moment I believed, and received the gospel."[12]

He would also claim, "Unless the almighty Arm had been under me I think I should have died with gratitude and joy. My eyes filled with tears and my voice was choked . . . I could only look up to heaven in silence, overwhelmed with love and wonder!"[13]

Cowper was thirty-three. Leaving the hospital to start life again, he met a family named Unwin. Around the fireside they would sit at prayer, and Cowper experienced a state of peace he had never thought possible. No man was an island; no man an exile.

When Mr. Unwin died, Cowper resettled with the rest of the family in the town of Olney. Does that name ring a bell? The local pastor happened to be John Newton. Quite naturally, the two men built a deep and abiding friendship. God had brought two stricken and stray sheep, two shipwrecked exiles, together. They were both willing captives of saving grace, and they both enjoyed pouring their devotion into hymns and poems. Cowper himself would go on to become one of England's greatest poets and men of letters. At one time he was considered for the position of England's poet laureate.

Together, William Cowper and John Newton produced the collection known as *Olney Hymns* in 1779. Of its 349 songs, sixty-seven were written by Cowper and all the rest by Newton. Grace abounds throughout the hymnal's pages, including in Cowper's well-known "God Moves in a Mysterious Way," and in the following familiar lines:

> *There is a fountain filled with blood*
> *Drawn from Immanuel's veins;*
> *And sinners, plunged beneath that flood,*
> *Lose all their guilty stains.*

> *The dying thief rejoiced to see*
> *That fountain in his day;*
> *And there have I, as vile as he,*
> *Washed all my sins away.*

E'er since by faith I saw the stream
Thy flowing wounds supply,
Redeeming love has been my theme,
And shall be till I die.

These men had found the fountain that is forever overflowing, the spring that wells up from eternity with everlasting life so that once men drink of it, they never thirst again. I hope you've found those waters and that you'll drink as deeply and gratefully of it today.

Moments *of* Grace

Have you been excusing a sin in your life by calling it another name? An unfortunate trait? A weakness? An unproductive habit? Before we can experience God's grace, we have to see ourselves as the sinners we really are in God's sight—as . . . well, as wretches. No, that's not the way society wants us to think of ourselves, but before we can experience abundant grace, we have to understand our total depravity and Christ's total love.

Consider writing out the words of 1 Timothy 1:13–14 and posting them where you can read them several times a day until they become personal to you: *I was formerly a blasphemer, a persecutor, and an insolent man [or woman]; but I obtained mercy. . . . And the grace of our Lord was exceedingly abundant . . .*

CHAPTER THREE

The Converting Power *of* Grace

I Once Was Lost but Now Am Found

A s Jesus sat down to teach, His eyes swept across the hodge-podge of humanity that was eagerly gathering around Him. As usual, it was neither the community's best nor its brightest who sought His wisdom today. Tax profiteers were here. Pleasure seekers were here. It was a representative assortment of the unwashed masses dismissively referred to as "sinners."

The religious leaders took their usual post on the periphery of the crowd—strategic placement for murmuring and whispering caustic commentary, also for avoiding dreaded physical contact with the ceremonially impure.

Then the world seemed to grow silent as the Master began to teach. Or rather to tell stories. The rabbi loved good narratives—long ones, short ones. This time He delivered His tales in a matching set, three variations on a theme. The subject might have been described as "lost and found."

First, there was a quick glimpse of a shepherd combing the rugged hills for a lost sheep, even to the point of neglecting ninety-nine others. Everyone could visualize the shepherd triumphantly bearing the bleating prize across his shoulders as his friends applauded.

Heaven, Jesus said, is something like those applauding shepherds. End of story.

Then He talked about a lost coin. This time the searcher was a frantic housekeeper, shaking every chair and pitcher to find that coin. Finally, with a little shriek of delight, the woman held high her prize. Like the shepherd, she couldn't help but call her friends and throw a party. There was a dash of humor in this story, and the crowd laughed appreciatively.

The angels, Jesus said, have such celebrations when even one sinner has a change of heart.

What must the Pharisees and scribes have made of all this—sheep and coins and clapping? What did misplaced possessions have to do with the Law of Moses? Purity—that was the issue, according to their Law! The only valid question was whether the shepherd or the woman were legally holy.

But Jesus wasn't finished for the day. Now He brought out the main course, to which the preceding dishes were mere appetizers. He told a story for the ages: one that echoes through history, that disarms every hearer, that no one ever tires of retelling. It is a story that loses nothing in any culture or setting, no matter where it is shared. Charles Dickens, the greatest of novelists in the English language, called this the greatest short story of all time.

This story concerned a lost son, but it was more than a quick sketch this time. With the skill of a masterful artist, Jesus painted the picture of the wealthy father of two young men, one of whom disgraces the family on an illicit spending spree. Each of the three main characters—father, elder son, lost son—will respond to the crisis in ways we would never quite have predicted. Yet when the story is complete, the hearer sits quietly and finally says, "Yes. The story is absolutely true. I know it is true because it is *my* story."

This is the power of the Prodigal. No one can help but see himself in the narrative. The painter Rembrandt was transfixed by the picture he found painted in the words of Luke 15. Early in his career, the artist was known to be an arrogant and pleasure-driven young man, and he painted himself into his version as the wandering son from the story, found in the shame of an Amsterdam brothel. Then, at the very end of his life, a wiser man but an ailing one, Rembrandt returned to the story again, this time painting himself into the parable as the loving father, embracing his child. Light emanates from the tender face of the father in a scene of raw emotional power.

The resulting masterpiece, *The Return of the Prodigal*, reached through the centuries to change the life of the Christian writer Henri Nouwen, who spent days silently meditating upon the spiritual resonance of the scene. As a result, Father Nouwen wrote a masterpiece of his own, a book named after the painting: *The Return of the Prodigal.*

Nouwen observes in his book that early in life, Rembrandt had responded, like many people, to the story of the son. As an older and wiser man, he sees the story in a new light. It has become for him a story not of the son who sins but of the father who forgives.

I believe Rembrandt and Nouwen were both on the right track.

FATHER OF MASTERPIECES

The story told by Jesus is a masterpiece that begets more masterpieces, in every medium. John Newton's "Amazing Grace" is one more in the list, because Newton saw himself as the world-wizened son who stumbled home. How could the words be chosen more simply or poignantly? *I once was lost but now am found.* He was that coin. He was that lamb. Above all, he was that wandering child who had brought shame to his birthright, who had committed acts his conscience would never turn loose. *Once lost; now found.* This is the story of all stories.

That other homeward-bound rebel, the apostle Paul, used the word *lost* only once in all his letters. But he, too, identified with the parable. Every sermon he preached in Acts and every epistle he wrote in our Bible echo with the themes of lost and found—of the helpless child captured by grace. Paul might well have seen himself everywhere in the story and even its setting: in the crowd that surrounded Jesus, among the scoffing Pharisees. He might have seen himself as the elder son, too proud of his own behavior to understand the grace he witnessed. In the end, of course, he had to join each one of us in identifying with the wandering, wasteful son. That identification is the needful step for every lost child in search of salvation.

We tend to focus on the player in this drama who carries the action—he who leaves, sins, and returns. Yet Rembrandt was absolutely right in placing the father at the center of the canvas. The Scriptures do no less, for the forgiving father is mentioned twelve times in twenty verses. He may go nowhere. He may "do" very little, at least visibly. But he is the true hero of this story, the true protagonist. We cannot understand any other character or any other development in this tale unless we see it through the eyes of that radiant father, without whom there is no story, no joy, no hope.

The Humiliation of the Father

A certain man had two sons. And the younger of them said to his father,
"Father, give me the portion of goods that falls to me." So he divided to them his livelihood.
—LUKE 15:11–12

There is nothing remarkable about the launch point of this parable: another restless young man with the cravings but not the capital. He lacks the maturity to respect the source of all that he has and all that he is. He simply wants what is coming to him.

Any young man would have known exactly where he stood. The Jewish Law made it clear and simple; you can read the fine print in Deuteronomy 21:17. In the case of two brothers, the older got two-thirds; the youngest got the rest. Either portion might be a nice fortune, but the catch was that the father needed to be dead first.

The second son's real message, then, is: "I can't wait for you to die, Dad."

Any normal father in that part of the world (or nearly any other part) would have slapped his son across the face and pushed him out on the doorstep—and he wouldn't have gotten any argument from the Jewish Law. But read between the lines of Luke, and you'll know very soon in the story that this is no common head of household. By the simple act of granting the insulting request, the father showed himself to be a man of grace.

This is a father who could see into the future. He knew the desolation and heartbreak that lay ahead for his son. He knew his own heartbreak. Yet he stood by the door and watched his son turn his back coldly and leave, taking with him one-third of the estate.

And what about that estate? We think in terms of stocks and bonds, the family silver, any real estate. The father in this story is clearly a man of means. We notice that his holdings included cattle and the acreage to keep them, servants and slaves, the ability to throw a great banquet at a moment's notice.

According to strict law, the father's land needn't be sold until his death. Again, a son late for distant parties would ignore such considerations. At the public sale of one-third of the land, every neighbor for miles would see into the family's shame.

In a small country with land at a premium, family inheritance was serious business. For the case of a young man who had lost his birthright among the Gentiles and dared to return home, a special ritual called the *kezazah* ("the cutting off") was established. According to Kenneth E. Bailey, the community would break a pot in front of the boy. They would cry out that the offender was cut off from his people and then turn their backs upon him forever.[2]

This wasn't a matter of sowing a few wild oats with the fallback plan of coming home later to take a place in the family business. This was a forever thing; a matter of drawing a line in the sand, insulting everyone on the other side, and disowning your people before they disown you. It was to say, "I invite you to ostracize me, and I don't care."

We place ourselves in the shoes of the father and wonder how we would respond. What emotions would dictate our actions? For many, the answer would be anger. Yet in this tale, the father's emotion is *disciplined love*. That kind of love has no strings, no conditions. It knowingly leaves every door open to hurt.

God's grace finds an expression infinitely repeated in His willingness to accept our insult. We stand before Him and say, "Give me what is mine," as if responsibility and obedience weren't part of the legacy. Who would want to take leave of His wonderful palace? Yet that's you and me. We go our way, to His heartbreak, until we have injured ourselves to our capacity of being injured.

God could take the stance of many parents and bar the doors, lock us in our rooms, and breed in us hearts of rebellion. Yet He stands and watches us set out on the path of misery, knowing it is the only way we will grow a heart of humble obedience. There is no limit to the mileage He will allow us to wander, no limit to the patience with which He awaits our return.

Paul the apostle and Newton the navigator understood just how far it was possible to travel before sailing off the edge of the world. For Paul, it was possible to take part in the murder of the saints. For

Newton, it was possible to assist in the enslavement of the innocent. For Paul, the far country was a few hidden rooms in Jerusalem. For Newton, the far country was the coast of Africa.

This particular distance is measured not in miles but in misery.

Separation from the Father

And not many days after, the younger son gathered all together, journeyed to a far country, and there wasted his possessions with prodigal living. But when he had spent all, there arose a severe famine in that land, and he began to be in want. Then he went and joined himself to a citizen of that country, and he sent him into his fields to feed swine. And he would gladly have filled his stomach with the pods that the swine ate, and no one gave him anything.

—LUKE 15:13–16

Cash in hand, the Prodigal sets out for the far country. Jesus gives it no name, because it's a place that is nowhere and everywhere. No matter who you are and where you live, there is a far country. No map is necessary. All you need is a sinful nature and a restless soul, and you are on your way.

For the son, that far country is all about sensuality, dissipation, and sexual adventurism—the cheapest bait Satan has to offer: "Eat, drink, and be merry." The problem with sensuality is that it fails to notice anything but the object of its lust. In this case, the Prodigal hasn't reckoned upon a local famine. Far earlier than he had imagined it (though he most likely never imagined it at all), his wallet runs dry.

Now he must turn from ceaseless partying to ceaseless labor. Poverty leaves him no choice. He finds himself working on the same sort of farm he has only recently liquidated. Every day he cannot help but see the true, enduring value of the land and the cattle.

But it is too late. He cannot bring back the estate he squandered—nor the love of the family he abandoned.

Manipulation of the Father

*But when he came to himself, he said, "How many of my father's hired servants have bread
enough and to spare, and I perish with hunger! I will arise and go to my father and will
say to him, 'Father, I have sinned against heaven and before you, and I am no longer
worthy to be called your son. Make me like one of your hired servants.' "*

—LUKE 15:17–19

For as many years as I have read and reflected and preached and
prayed over this parable, I have been drawn to three words in this
passage. Those three words change the whole course of the story.

The three words come when the Prodigal *came to himself.*

What exactly happened when he "came to himself"? I've heard
many sermons that fix upon that phrase as the moment of grace. We
imagine that the Prodigal feels deep conviction for the sins he has committed, and we imagine him going to his knees to confess and repent.

Frankly, that's a stretch.

Read the passage again and look for any word such as *sorry* or
remorseful. Is it all about his guilty soul, or is it actually about his
empty stomach? Does he sincerely repent, or does he just have good
common sense about getting a square meal?

We cannot be certain of the answer—or, more to the point, Jesus
keeps it dark. For in a parable we see exactly what the Master desires
us to see. And what He wants us to know for now is that the Prodigal knows he needs help. He surrenders. If there is any slim hope of
his reinstatement at home, then at the very least he must repay every
cent he has squandered. Working as a pig farmer, he knows he will
never make it that far. As a matter of fact, he hasn't even been paid
for his labor ("No one gave him anything" [v. 16]). He only thought
that slopping hogs was reaching the bottom; slopping them for
free—even lower.

So now he is desperate enough to consider slinking home. He sees himself at the very bottom of the pecking order, no longer a son but a servant. In time, maybe over a number of years, he could work off his debt.

It is essential that we, Jesus' listeners, understand that the Prodigal is still unprepared for grace. He is still running his own plans, only sadder and wiser in running them. Whether he realizes it or not, he is still securely within the borders of the far country, a self-chosen exile from the rescue of unconditional love.

We might prefer that the Prodigal "redeem himself," but that would be a misunderstanding of this parable and a misunderstanding of grace. No one on this planet has the ability to redeem him- or herself. Every one of us, like the Prodigal, must ultimately throw him- or herself on the mercy of the court.

But wait—are we *certain* the Prodigal isn't penitent? Listen to his speech he is preparing to give: "Father, I have sinned against heaven and before you, and I am no longer worthy to be called your son."

Again, Kenneth Bailey offers us a surprising glimpse behind the details. The Pharisees in Jesus' audience would recognize the son's speech as the words of Pharaoh when he tried to manipulate Moses into lifting the plagues (see Exodus 10:16). The Egyptian ruler certainly had no contrite heart; his words were simply damage control for the natural disasters that were ravaging his land. He would have said whatever Moses wanted him to say.[3]

Many a humble word has been spoken when someone is at the mercy of someone else. Words are cheap and inadmissible as evidence of a repentant heart. The Prodigal was simply seeking access to what he hadn't already consumed of his father's estate.

In other words, he is like you or me trying to save ourselves, completely on our own.

Reconciliation with the Father

And he arose and came to his father. But when he was still a great way off,
his father saw him and had compassion, and ran and fell on his neck and kissed him.
And the son said to him, "Father, I have sinned against heaven and in your sight,
and am no longer worthy to be called your son."
—LUKE 15:20–21

My mind's eye has always held a vivid image of this scene. I cannot imagine a picture more laden with emotion.

Here is the Prodigal, clad in shredded rags that had once been the high fashion of the moment. He is far thinner than anyone remembers him. His beard is clotted with dust, and his hair falls unkempt over his sagging shoulders. Like vagabonds everywhere, he clutches his meager possessions in a greasy sack, and he bears the odors of desperate alleys. Perhaps during the last few moments he has walked past old acquaintances, boyhood friends, and servants who failed to recognize him.

But the father doesn't even hesitate. He knows his boy immediately, because he has been watching, ever vigilant. His grieving imagination has already worked out how his son would appear on that glorious day of his return.

From the Greek text, we know that the father was not indoors when this storm-beaten scarecrow appeared on the horizon. The patriarch was out keeping watch, as a shepherd would do for a lost sheep, as a woman would do for the lost circle of silver. The father walks down this road each day, as far as he might safely venture from his estate, propelled only by hope for the reunion upon which he has set his heart. We know that he kept watch with all that was in him, for that is the essence of all three stories Jesus tells in Luke 15—a relentless pursuit of the lost treasure.

The father, then, sees the shell of his son from a distance, and he is consumed by compassion. He takes in the labored steps, the bent posture, the very picture of weary surrender, and there is no room in the father's heart for any substance but love. So joyful, so uncontrollable is the emotion within him that he begins to run toward the figure—even to "race," we are told. This would be unseemly for a Middle Eastern man of his estate. Everything was to be done with quiet dignity. To run means taking up his mantle in his hand, so that he won't stumble. It means exposing his bare legs. All of these things are beneath the pride of a patriarch. But true love is a powerful force. It erupts on occasion. It is totally unself-conscious.

If the sincerity of the son is ambiguous, there can be no mistake about the heart of the father. And that touches upon the very essence of this parable. The power comes from the father's grace, not the son's guilt.

There is still, however, the issue of public shame—for the boy and his clan. The father is more than aware of that. Therefore he humbles himself in running. He meets the boy in stride. He enfolds him in the full acceptance of his embrace, and he takes on his child's humiliation by his very body language.[4]

Try to imagine the story otherwise. We might yet have been moved if the son knocked at the door, went down on his knees, and had his apology gruffly accepted by the father. We might call it justice tempered by mercy. But nothing of the kind happens here. Instead, the father commits himself fully before a word can leave the mouth of his son, before the son can come across the property, before the son could even be recognized by anyone other than a parent who brought him into the world. The son's carefully prepared speech will be delivered as planned, but only after he has been showered in joy, grace, and kisses. By this time, the speech is neither rote nor rigid. The Prodigal is a helpless child again, secure in his father's arms with no need to plan or contrive. Only now is repentance genuine, when it floats upon a sea of grace.

There at the very edge of the village, a supernatural event has taken place. On this spot, grace has overwhelmed guilt. The Prodigal has come to that place as a lost person. He has not found himself any more than the sheep or the coin found themselves. In all cases, it took the obsessive love of the searcher for the lost thing to be redeemed.

The primary miracle is the insistence of grace. A secondary miracle is the thawing of a frozen heart. Even the selfish, calculating Prodigal cannot withstand the sight of his running, weeping father surrendering his high position to meet him at the edge of disgrace. In that moment grace takes him captive, and he sees what his rebellious soul has not until now allowed him to see: the beauty of his father's love, the absolute value of his acceptance, the sweet joys of loyalty and obedience. As far as his conscience goes, no one need tell him the depth of the pain he has brought to his home. He knows it now not simply with his mind but in the furthest depths of his heart.

That heart is broken, yet his soul is mended. Such is the supernatural event of grace.

Celebration of the Father

> But the father said to his servants, "Bring out the best robe and put it on him,
> and put a ring on his hand and sandals on his feet. And bring the fatted
> calf here and kill it, and let us eat and be merry; for this my son was dead
> and is alive again; he was lost and is found." And they began to be merry.
>
> —LUKE 15:22–24

Joy cares nothing for solitude. Somehow it always wants to invite a few friends.

There are so many things the Prodigal wants to say at this moment, so many things he *must* say to his father. Yet his father seems to be in no hurry to hear the lurid details of history or the fine print of confession. He is whirling in every direction, calling servants and grabbing slaves by the elbow. He sees in his mind a party such as never has been thrown in these parts.

Once it was the son who was so impatient for parties. The roles have reversed. The father wants the most expensive clothing in the house, the finest jewelry, the most elegant shoes. He insists upon the prime cut of the best beef that can be found on the ranch.

Every command is a meaningful expression of love to his son. The best robe would be the father's own, and that would signify the son's complete restoration to the family. The ring was a symbol of business, used to imprint wax and seal a deal. The ring said, "You are part of our daily operations. You may transact business on our behalf." The shoes squelched any possibility of the son returning as a servant. Only the family wore shoes. The fatted calf was simply an expression of deep joy—the best course for the happiest event.

As Jesus has said earlier, "There is joy in the presence of the angels of God over one sinner who repents" (Luke 15:10). Now we have the earthly picture of that joy.

Condemnation of the Father

Now his older son was in the field. And as he came and drew near to the house, he heard music and dancing. So he called one of the servants and asked what these things meant. And he said to him, "Your brother has come, and because he has received him safe and sound, your father has killed the fatted calf." But he was angry and would not go in. Therefore his father came out and pleaded with him. So he answered and said to his father, "Lo, these many years I have been serving you; I never transgressed your commandment at any time; and yet you never gave

me a young goat, that I might make merry with my friends. But as soon as this son
of yours came, who has devoured your livelihood with harlots, you killed the fatted
calf for him." And he said to him, "Son, you are always with me, and all that I
have is yours. It was right that we should make merry and be glad, for your
brother was dead and is alive again, and was lost and is found."

—LUKE 15:25–32

So compelling is the interplay between this father and son that we are often taken by surprise when a third character walks onto the stage. As we knew from the beginning, there is an older son. He is the heir who stands to inherit two-thirds of the estate. He has bided his time and paid his dues in the family business.

When little brother came home, the older son was not there. We can only imagine him approaching the homestead after a long day of supervising the activities on a ranch. What is this music drifting across the lawn? What is the laughter and happy shouting coming from a habitually quiet estate?

A servant scurries by on some errand, and the older son takes him aside for questioning. The servant fills him in: "It's your brother—he's back, and your father is throwing the bash to end all bashes!"

The young fellow hurries on, and the brother stands there, trying to process what he has heard. *Can this be? My little brother is not dead after all? And why would our father throw a party for someone who destroyed our name and went through a third of our wealth?*

But for the most part, it's not really about *we*. It's about *me*. The more he thinks about it, the angrier and more self-righteous the older brother becomes. By the time he confronts his father, he is refusing to even call the guest of honor a brother. He is "this son of yours" (v. 30). And the message is, "Is this what you call justice? Rewarding a disgrace and ignoring loyalty?"

I have come to two conclusions about this older brother.

1. *He was a son who was living like a servant.* "Lo, these many years I have been serving you" (v. 29). Has he been doing it for love, or was it just good business? Go back to verse 12, and you might be surprised to discover that the father didn't just give the younger brother his share; he gave *both* sons what they had coming to them. When the father said, "All that I have is yours," he was simply stating what had become fact some time back. The older brother was a wealthy young man—not only in hard cash but in the love of his father. Unfortunately, somewhere along the line, he had *become* his work. He was all about earning, proving. Grace made no sense to him.

2. *The older brother was a sinner who thought he was a saint.* He says, "I never transgressed your commandment" (v. 29). Oh, really? That's a bit hard for us to imagine. There is no such thing as a perfect son. In some sense, every son or daughter among us is a prodigal. The older brother may have never left the estate, but he had still fled to the far country of pride and self-righteousness—much like Paul, who never left Jerusalem. Remember, prodigal distance is measured not in miles but in misery. The older son appears to be every bit as miserable as his brother. In fact, he refuses to enter the house where the party is in full swing (v. 28).

That's one of the saddest lines in Scripture. One son was so far from obedience, yet he basked in grace. The other was little *but* obedient, and he never received the priceless treasure that was within his reach all along.

How many of us share a frightening resemblance to that older brother? How about you? Could that gift be right there before you even now? Maybe you didn't travel to the Prodigal's den of sensuality. You might have taken the room right next door, where you found the dungeon of grim obedience. In this story, that was the harder one to escape.

These are two sides of the same coin: law and licentiousness. Either one makes slaves, and only in grace is liberation possible.

LOST AND FOUND

Jesus finishes His trilogy and looks up at the crowd. Before Him are the so-called sinners—prodigals all. Many of them are visibly moved: faces wet or hidden in hands. More than a few are openly weeping. How could they *not* have identified with a character who broke every rule, spat in the face of all that was good and true, and somehow received love rather than condemnation? This is like no story they've ever heard. Could God really be like that father?

Beyond that layer of listeners, Jesus watches for the reaction of the older brothers—the scribes and Pharisees, grimly obedient laborers who pay endless dues on the ranches of Mosaic Law.

What Jesus sees does not surprise Him. Smugness. Smirking. Educated as they are, many of them probably don't identify with the character in the story who so clearly took their part. The self-righteous are like that—amazingly incapable of looking into the mirror of self-inspection.

Jesus has told these stories very deliberately. As He prepared to teach, He couldn't help but hear the mumbled criticisms about how He'd been spending His time—dining with sinners! Socializing with tax collectors! Imagine.

So He has told two stories that answer the question, "What is the value of the lost thing?"

First He has spoken of a sheep, which has reasonable value. The shepherd will go out of his way to find it.

Then He has spoken of a coin, with more buying power than a lamb. Therefore the woman will comb the house with proportionate urgency.

Then, after these sample problems, Jesus has brought the final exam. If a sheep has a value of x, and a silver coin has a value of, say, $10x$—then what value is carried by a misplaced soul? Is it $1,000x$?

$1,000,000x$? No mathematics can express such a sum. It would crash the theological computer.

That was one they didn't teach in Pharisee school. The value of Law they understood; the value of humanity was simply off topic.

Jesus said, in essence, "Here is the answer to the question. The rescue of one lost soul is worth more than the gold of a billion galaxies; therefore, it is cause for angelic celebration. The rescue of one lost soul brings the Creator of the universe Himself thundering down the path to embrace you. It sets off a celebration that never ends. It restores the lost soul to its family. It affords the soul the right to transact work for the kingdom. It invites the reign of love and grace, so that no sin you've ever committed even enters the equation. That is the value of one lost soul."

And Jesus might well have added, "You Pharisees have more facts about God than anyone. You are walking encyclopedias of holiness. You know what you need to do. As for Me, I'm here to keep watch on that lonely road, at the edge of the village, that highway to the far country. I know the name of every soul who wanders that road. I know the pain of every heartache they feel. And I am here to tell them what you will not tell them. I am here to put a robe of pure white upon their shoulders, to hide their sodden rags forever. And I am here to lay down My life and take on every stroke of punishment they have earned, because I can bear it and they cannot.

"After that, if you will but walk through this open door—we'll throw parties that put the far country to shame."

Moments *of* Grace

Which character in the story of the Prodigal Son is most like you? Are you a parent grieved over the sin of another? Are you yourself a backslider and a wayward soul? A responsible citizen yet filled with silent resentment like the older brother? Or is it possible you're a combination of all three?

Whatever your condition, remind yourself that you are worth more to God than the gold of a billion galaxies. He is seeking you, waiting for you, watching over you, and wanting to lead you to new levels of joy, peace, and strength. Today, begin your prayer to the Lord with these words: "Dear Lord, I am just like . . ." and name your character. Tell the Lord all about it, and feel the uplift of His loving grace.

CHAPTER FOUR

The Clear Perspective of Grace

Was Blind, but Now I See

In an age of instant gratification, nearly everything has become available at rapid speed. You can receive an e-mail from the other side of the world only a second or two after it was composed, rather than waiting for an old-fashioned stamped letter to work its way through the world's labyrinthine postal system. You can shed those ugly pounds in seven days. You can see a photograph in the handy viewer *before* the lens snaps.

But a few things must still be brought to a slow simmer. Authentic, inside-out change is one of those things. Salvation is the ultimate version of a "new you." Having been told that you are a new creation, you expect to rise and walk in newness of life.

Why, then, do we have this creeping suspicion that nothing has really changed? Why do we still struggle with so many challenges in life: hasty words, compulsive habits, seductive temptations? Why don't we feel the moment-by-moment desire to be all the wonderful things Christ has promised us we can be?

Take heart. Every single one of us who answers to the name of Christian is a fellow struggler in this regard. There is no "microwave" serving of spiritual maturity. We all have to "work out [our] own salvation with fear and trembling" (Philippians 2:12).

Case in point: John Newton.

Those who love the story of Newton sometimes imagine him experiencing his moment of grace onboard his slave ship. They imagine the newly enlightened believer turning the ship back to return the slaves, as he quickly sits down to pen the verses to "Amazing Grace."

History tells another story: a story of the slave trader docking in Liverpool and then promptly signing himself on for another voyage to Africa. There he traveled from slave factory to slave factory, buying slaves and storing them in his ship, just like always. He sailed for the New World and studied his Bible as two hundred slaves were packed into shelving in the hold beneath him. On many voyages, as many as one-third of these men, women, and children died. Many others developed serious illnesses. Newton disembarked from the voyage and enjoyed the fresh air and outlying fields of Charleston, South Carolina, as the remaining slaves went to market and to their eventual destinies on rice plantations. Newton wouldn't write "Amazing Grace" until twenty-five years after his conversion.

Lest you find these facts shocking, it's important to understand the historical context. At the time, most believers did not see slavery as evil. The truth is that Newton spent ten years as a slave trader, and most of those came after his salvation.

Yet the committed believer begins to hear the voice of the Holy Spirit more clearly as time goes by. He begins to see the world as the Father sees it and to think with the mind of Christ. John Newton experienced a dawning horror about the true evil of his former vocation. His friends began to notice how often he discussed his qualms about the slave business.

The fact was that the old John Newton and the new one were two different men—and the new one was beginning to find his voice.

In 1788, Newton published a ten-thousand-word confessional pamphlet, *Thoughts upon the African Slave Trade.* Here he came clean as an opponent of the practice as old as humanity. He confessed his own part in years of the trade and realized there was nothing he could do now to repay the evil in which he had taken part. "I hope it will always be a subject of humiliating reflection to me," he wrote, "that I was once an active instrument in a business at which my heart now shudders."

As he approached death many years later, Newton would claim that much of his memory was fading. "But I remember two things," he wrote. "That I am a great sinner, and that Christ is a great Savior."[1] He held on to the two essential facts. Penitence is the prelude to the wonderful work of grace.

EYES WIDE SHUT

I remember planning an evening worship service several years ago. We would be coming to the Lord's table for Communion and then having the sermon. I realized with alarm that my text was Romans 1:29–32: twenty-one words cataloguing the corruption and depravity of humanity, perhaps the darkest pit to be found in Scripture. There was something terribly wrong about descending into this pit following the elevating moment of Communion.

The worst thing I could have done would have been to back away from the insistence of God's Word. Instead, I simply changed the order of service. I preached those troubling verses from Romans, and *then* we came to the table. As a result, there was a miracle within our fellowship. The experience of God's presence that evening was overwhelming. I saw the kind of tears I had rarely seen over the sharing of the elements. I certainly had to restrain my own emotions in order to preside.

How could a mere revamped order of worship make such a difference? On the next day I found out. It was Monday morning, and I happened to be reading a book called *Not the Way It's Supposed to Be: A Breviary of Sin.* The author, Cornelius Plantinga Jr., made the point that we seriously delude ourselves about the presence of evil in our lives. It's like purposefully removing all the black keys from the piano. Once you do that, the white keys no longer produce a melody. If we edit the sin out of our awareness, then grace no longer has any beauty or power for us. In due time we wonder why we need a Savior at all.[2]

In our worship service on the preceding evening, we happened to have gotten it right. We faced the reality of sin at full force, letting the Spirit of God do His gentle task of application within every soul present. When we came to the Lord's table, we experienced the most powerful working of His presence and grace we could have imagined. His body, broken for us; His blood, spilled for us—these were no longer theoretical concepts but realities that cut deep in the context of the very real sin that had been brought to our awareness.

Then again, I'm not naive enough to believe that everyone present shared in the experience. The voice of God himself may come in loud and clear, yet there are always those who aren't tuned in to the right frequency. I think of the struggler in the temple, pouring out his confession, as the Pharisee nearby observes him and prays, "Lord, I thank You that I am not like that sinner over there" (Luke 18:9–14). Surely there were those in our sanctuary who heard the menu of sins in Romans and applied them to everyone but themselves.

As Mark McMinn puts it, "Part of our mess is not knowing we are a mess."[3] We live quiet lives, never robbing a bank or committing a murder. None of us has been employed as a slave trader or held the robes of those throwing rocks at a martyr. We confuse calmness with holiness. It's been observed in surveys that the average person believes he is better than the average person.[4] We are blind to our own blindness.

It is the Pharisee in the temple, smug in his assumed righteousness, who concerns Paul in the second chapter of his letter to the Romans. He has known a lot of those; he had been one himself. He began his letter to the Romans with a powerful sermon against the clear-cut wickedness of the world. Any Jewish leader would have been standing and applauding, shouting "amen" to every sentence, every condemnation. They loved hearing him go after those worldly Gentiles.

But then they would have come to the next section—Romans 2. The amen corner would fall into shocked silence. For now, Paul was pointing an accusing finger at the "righteous." He used the same two words to sum up their position before God: "without excuse" (Romans 1:20).

The Jews of the time saw themselves walking proudly in the light of God's favoritism, while the blind Gentiles around them stumbled. No wonder they were no fans of Jesus when He told them that they, too, were blind—the blind leading the blind, as He described it. That combination, He said, ends up with everyone lying in the ditch (Luke 6:39).

EYES WIDE OPEN

The word that best describes Paul's opening to Romans 2 is *diatribe*. This was an argument presented through a lively debate with a heckler, real or imagined. Paul mastered the technique through his

travels, bringing new and unaccepted ideas into traditional synagogues. Someone might call out, "Ha! Here's the problem with your
theory . . ." And Paul would engage his challenger—a kind of show-
business technique for dealing with abstract ideas. Think of two
professional wrestlers on TV, hurling aggressive theological taunts.

Paul's stance was something like this: "So you think you're high
and mighty, that you're God's fair-haired boy? You'd better buy lightning insurance, and here's why."

The "why" turns out to be *judgment.* Paul uses some form of that
word seven times in three verses.

More important, in sixteen verses he presents six principles for
self-examination. Like Jonathan Edwards's classic sermon "Sinners in
the Hands of an Angry God," these verses refuse to candy-coat the
truth. They present the idea that your vision may be clouded, but
rest assured that God's eyesight is twenty-twenty. "And there is no
creature hidden from His sight, but all things are naked and open to
the eyes of Him to whom we must give account" (Hebrews 4:13).

God's Judgment Is According to Reality

Therefore you are inexcusable, O man, whoever you are who judge,
for in whatever you judge another you condemn yourself;
for you who judge practice the same things.
—ROMANS 2:1

That's how the New King James Version translates it. Donald Grey
Barnhouse created his own wording for this verse: "You dummy—
do you really figure that you have doped out an angle that will let
you go up against God and get away with it? You don't have a ghost
of a chance."[5]

That's what we mean by a diatribe, and it would get most preachers fired these days. But Paul brings such passion to this subject as one could only have when he has been there and done that himself. He assumes that if these folks are sight-impaired, he'd better write in big letters; if they are deaf, he'd better shout. As we read these verses in the Bible and really comprehend what is being said, our fingers almost feel singed by the page.

The hypocrite, Paul tells us, is totally intolerant of anyone's sins but his own. But what is most striking is the idea found in Shakespeare's *Hamlet*, "The lady doth protest too much, methinks." In other words, the louder you shout, the more likely it is that you are attempting to draw attention away from yourself. Your condemnations, according to Paul, really condemn *you*.

We call it hypocrisy. Paul is saying, "You're guilty of everything you criticize."

But surely that label wouldn't apply to you and me, would it? You watched those looters after the hurricanes and felt righteous indignation—and you're not guilty of looting. You saw a TV documentary about the spread of sexual permissiveness, and you were disgusted—and you haven't engaged in such licentiousness. You cheered when they caught that murderer—but you've resisted the temptation to kill anyone, even that neighbor down the street who really makes your blood boil! As a matter of fact, you'd like to . . .

Wait a minute: maybe *that's* what Paul is talking about.

Jesus told us during the Sermon on the Mount that our anger amounts to murder, that our lust amounts to adultery, and that basically we stand convicted upon our innermost thoughts.

Now there's a frightening idea. Imagine the crime-scene investigators combing your innermost thoughts for evidence. Who among us would be righteous? Therefore, yes, Paul can say, "You who judge practice the same things." And yes, it applies to you and to me and to the religious elite who were the targets of Paul's diatribe.

God's Judgment Is According to Integrity

*But we know that the judgment of God is according to truth against those who
practice such things. And do you think this, O man, you who judge those practicing
such things, and doing the same, that you will escape the judgment of God?*

—ROMANS 2:2–3

How many of us let John Newton off the hook for trading slaves? I
know I did. After all (we remind ourselves), he lived in an unenlight-
ened age. He simply fell in with the crowd.

How, then, do people living within the biases of their times manage to take two giant steps ahead of the crowd and proclaim something wrong, even when the world says it is right? Newton did it. So
did a few others of his time. What is the source of that insistent voice
that overrides the entire social conscience of our era? The mere whisper of the Holy Spirit can drown out the thundering noise of an
entire world. Newton came to a place where he could dare to stand
back and look upon his former livelihood and condemn it. How
many of us would have had such courage? Probably none without
the sustaining strength of that Spirit.

"For the LORD does not see as man sees; for man looks at the
outward appearance, but the LORD looks at the heart" (1 Samuel
16:7). Paul has made this very point in Romans 1. In the words of
Eugene Peterson's paraphrase, *The Message*, "By taking a long and
thoughtful look at what God has created, people have always been
able to see what their eyes as such can't see. . . . So nobody has a good
excuse" (Romans 1:20).

For Christians, the voice of the Spirit takes precedence. But even
for those who have never heard the Gospel, there is a conscience that
is issued as standard equipment in the human engine.

The judgment of God takes the measure of our integrity, so no one can say, "Everybody was doing it." No soldier of the cross can say, "I was simply acting under orders," unless the orders in fact come from that voice of authority God has placed within His followers.

God's Judgment Is According to Opportunity

Or do you despise the riches of His goodness, forbearance, and longsuffering, not knowing that the goodness of God leads you to repentance? But in accordance with your hardness and your impenitent heart you are treasuring up for yourself wrath in the day of wrath and revelation of the righteous judgment of God.

—ROMANS 2:4–5

"Listen," Paul says. "You upright, moral citizens have been enjoying the luxury of every possible advantage—and you dismiss them as if they were nothing by sinning against God."

What advantages? Paul names three: God's kindness, His forbearance, and His patience. These are all expressions of an infinite love that can never be deserved, could never be earned, and *certainly* should never be taken for granted.

Consider this world, teeming with people who lived and died without being told the first fact about Jesus Christ. The immeasurable wealth of His teachings and the liberating knowledge of His death and resurrection were unknown to them. They lived and died in darkness.

Meanwhile, we are those who live in the light. The full testimony of God's revelation and the full counsel of His kindness have been available to us all along, yet we dishonor Him. Unread Bibles collect dust on our shelves, when there are those in other countries who would give all that they own for one ragged New Testament.[6]

The kindness of God shed upon you and me is as unmistakable as the sun on a summer day, as prevalent as the oxygen in the air. How can we live as if we were utterly independent of His goodness?

Or how can we describe people so heedless of God's greatest favor? Paul calls their problem "hardness" or stubbornness (v. 5). The word in Greek is *sklerotes*, which is the source of our medical word *sclerosis*. Arteriosclerosis is the hardening of the arteries, in the case of the physical heart. But we speak of a spiritual heart; and it, too, has arteries that may harden. What can bring about such a condition? There would be many answers, but this much we can agree upon: anyone who is capable of ignoring God's kindness, patience, and forbearance is a chronic sufferer from that condition.

God's Judgment Is According to Morality

Who "will render to each one according to his deeds": eternal life to those who by patient continuance in doing good seek for glory, honor, and immortality; but to those who are self-seeking and do not obey the truth, but obey unrighteousness—indignation and wrath, tribulation and anguish, on every soul of man who does evil, of the Jew first and also of the Greek; but glory, honor, and peace to everyone who works what is good, to the Jew first and also to the Greek.

—ROMANS 2:6–10

Jesus said, "The Son of Man will come in the glory of His Father with His angels, and then He will reward each according to his works" (Matthew 16:27). As a matter of fact, your Bible is packed with reminders that an hour of accounting is coming. If your Bible were an appointment book (as in a way it is), it would have yellow Post-it notes falling from every page, reminding you to be ready for your appointment with destiny. If your Bible were a clock (as in a way it is), its alarm would be sounding every few minutes to remind you to start getting ready. But you and I tend to hit the snooze button. We mumble, "Just a few more moments to relax."

Paul's comment on that day of judgment is this: You get no

credit for the number of Bibles you own. The test of accountability will not be a "sword drill" in which we prove how many verses we have memorized. The test will instead be an inspection of how thoroughly those scriptures have permeated our lives. It will be a fruit inspection: what has blossomed from the buds of your allotted years on this planet?

It is obedience to God, not the knowledge of Him, that will make or break us. As a matter of fact, we could actually be worse off for being the sword-drill champion. For "disobeying the law which is being constantly dinned into one's ears will make condemnation so much more severe."[7]

God's Judgment Is According to Impartiality

For there is no partiality with God. For as many as have sinned without law
will also perish without law, and as many as have sinned in the law will be judged
by the law (for not the hearers of the law are just in the sight of God, but the doers
of the law will be justified; for when Gentiles, who do not have the law, by nature
do the things in the law, these, although not having the law, are a law to themselves,
who show the work of the law written in their hearts, their conscience also bearing witness,
and between themselves their thoughts accusing or else excusing them).
—ROMANS 2:11–15

In his book *Mere Christianity*, C. S. Lewis makes the same observation that Paul sets out in this passage. Isn't it interesting, Paul remarks, how all these Gentiles imitate so many aspects of the Hebrew Law, even though they've never heard it? They "show the work of the law written in their hearts, their conscience also bearing witness" (v. 15).

As for Lewis, he points out that in the midst of an argument, you will notice that people appeal to some standard of fairness. They say,

"How would you like that if someone did it to you?" Or, "I helped you, so you should help me." Take any atheist and he will appeal regularly to universal standards, the same as anyone else. Every time he says, "That's not fair," he has just condemned his own philosophy.

The revealing point is that when we make these appeals to standards, no one ever disputes their existence. They may try to find loopholes, but they never say, "There are no standards. There is no right or wrong." If we really believed there weren't rules, Lewis says, we would have no recourse but to pounce upon each other like beasts and thrash it out. Instead, we quarrel—and quarreling cannot occur unless someone has established rules to govern the dispute.[8]

Even the godless show "the work of the law written in their hearts" (v. 15). No matter how freethinking they may believe themselves to be, their consciences keep bearing witness.

God's Judgment Is According to Certainty

In the day when God will judge the secrets of men by Jesus Christ, according to my gospel.
—ROMANS 2:16

The Lord searches every heart and understands every intention, according to 1 Chronicles 28:9. How foolish must we be to bargain with Him, to posture before Him, or to speak to Him in any manner that is not absolute sincerity? The Spirit of God dwells among the file cabinets of your mind. He knows the inventory of the hairs on your head and the hours, minutes, and seconds of your life. Truly understanding the implications of that, we would be taken by uncontrollable fear if His character were not kind, patient, and forbearing. Who else could we trust with the contents of those file cabinets? Who else but someone with absolutely perfect, infinitely unconditional love?

Yet we go about the pretense of having any thought squirreled

away from the eyes of God. Søren Kierkegaard, a Danish philosopher of the nineteenth century, watched a sixteen-year-old girl on
her confirmation day. She was showered with gifts, among them a
New Testament in a decorative binding.

Kierkegaard reflected upon the fact that no one really expected
the girl to ever read the Bible; it was basically given as an ornament,
a social prop. At the very best, the intention of the giver would be
that if the girl ever found herself in emotional need, the Testament
might come in handy. Yet within the bounds of such a life, the
philosopher concluded, a true reading of those Scriptures would provide anything but comfort—they would suggest far greater terrors
than whatever brought her to open the pages in the first place.

Kierkegaard's conclusion is that rather than live such a dangerous
hypocrisy, we should walk through the town, take up every single
Bible, and cart the whole load out to some mountaintop where we
can say to God, "Take it back, this book! We are only capable of
making ourselves miserable with it!"[9]

For the prophet Ezekiel, it is as if we sit in church with stupid
grins and enjoy the cadence of the preacher's speaking, the lilt of his
voice, and the fine sound of the Bible translation he has chosen. In
other words, it has all become music without lyrics to us. It is the
Word of God as elevator music, full of sound and fury and signify-
ing nothing. As the prophet puts it, "Indeed you are to them as a
very lovely song of one who has a pleasant voice and can play well
on an instrument; for they hear your words, but they do not do
them" (Ezekiel 33:32).

Lord, deliver us from such self-inflicted emptiness. Maybe
Kierkegaard is right—maybe it would be better to give back our
Bibles than to let them become frilly ornaments to unexamined lives.
Help us to hear every eternal, inspired fragment of truth that issues
from the revelation of the Word of God. Help us to look upon every

detail of that which the Spirit would have us see. Otherwise we are blind indeed—one long procession of blind people, happily leading each other to a ditch as deep as the pits of fire.

We could be as blind as the characters in Hans Christian Anderson's tale "The Emperor's New Clothes." The king loved beautiful clothing, but he was as gullible as he was vain. Inevitably he became the prey of con men who promised to weave him a suit of thread so rare that only the pure in heart could see it. The emperor paid a fortune for his new suit, and the hucksters pretended to be weaving industriously. None of the royal advisers would admit that they couldn't see any thread on the loom. They gave glowing reports of the beauty of the clothing.

The whole charade culminated in the crafty weavers "dressing" the naked emperor in his brand-new attire. Then they skipped town with the proceeds. An announcement was made: There would be a royal parade, and only the pure in heart should attend. For only they could appreciate the special clothing the emperor would wear.

Attendance was high, since everyone believed him- or herself to fit the criteria. But who would give voice to the spectacle their eyes took in? It took a young child to blow the lid off the whole scam. He loudly proclaimed that the emperor had no clothes.[10]

In Romans 2, Paul has become that child. He goes to the fashion show of holiness and says that he sees nothing but naked moralists. But the message never goes over well. People would rather not be awakened from their illusion. We desperately want to *see* those beautiful threads. We want to hear soothing music when the Word of God is proclaimed. We want to look at our own chests and see them covered with medals for every achievement in spiritual purity, above and beyond the call of duty, so that there is no day of judgment at all; instead, the hosts of heaven will throw a testimonial banquet in our honor.

The scales fell away from John Newton's eyes, but only after years of inner struggle. He had to learn to see and to hear. He had to learn to think with the mind of Christ. Praise God that the day could come when he could sing out, "I once . . . was blind, but now I see."

Paul, too, rose from the ground after his incident on the road to Damascus. He dusted himself off and reflected on the words of Christ that had just thundered down upon him from heaven. Yet there was no instant sainthood delivered by angelic courier. To underscore his neediness, God struck him blind. He was utterly dependent upon a certain man in a certain town to care for him. For Paul, blindness was one of the requirements for sight.

The Holy Spirit will not let you be content in your blindness. He would not allow it for Paul, nor would He allow it for John Newton. Be assured He will not allow it for you. He longs to open the curtains and let in the light that will make your world sparkle with all the bright colors of paradise.

Only beware—it takes awhile for our eyes to become accustomed when the light floods into a darkened room. Even the beauty of pure light is painful at first. But even at that moment, even when our spiritual nakedness is laid painfully bare, we know that our shame is only momentary. We know that we are clothed in the grace that overwhelms every blemish.

In the words of Clara H. Scott's hymn:

> *Open my eyes, that I may see*
> *Glimpses of truth Thou hast for me;*
> *Place in my hands the wonderful key*
> *That shall unclasp and set me free.*
> *Silently now I wait for Thee,*
> *Ready, my God, Thy will to see;*
> *Open my eyes, illumine me, Spirit divine!*

Moments *of* Grace

This chapter warns that we seriously delude ourselves about the presence of evil in our lives. By nature we're not tuned to the divine frequency, and we're like the self-justifying Pharisee in Luke 18:9–14, not realizing the mess we're in.

As you conclude this chapter, pray earnestly—you might even kneel or take a moment to write out these words as a covenant to God—Psalm 139:23–24: "Search me, O God, and know my heart; try me, and know my anxieties; and see if there is any wicked way in me, and lead me in the way everlasting."

But beware! If you make that your earnest prayer before the Lord, be ready! God wants to shine the spotlight of His Spirit into your life to show you elements of attitude and behavior that need to be confessed and repented. It may be discouraging at first, but the result will be a richer life with a greater understanding of His astounding grace.

CHAPTER FIVE

The Comforting Provision *of* Grace

*'Twas Grace That Taught My Heart to Fear
and Grace My Fears Relieved*

E V. Hill was a gifted preacher of the Gospel. An African-American who was literally born in a log cabin, he started a church in the middle of the explosive Watts district of Los Angeles, and all his life he made a difference.

I'll never forget the day I heard him deliver a sermon at a conference at the Moody Bible Institute. The title was "What Do You Have if You Have Jesus?" Every one of his twelve sermon points came to life in the power of illustrations I could still produce from memory today. He held us spellbound.

As the pastor explained a particular point about blessings, he reached over to a little table stacked with award books to be handed out later. Dr. Hill was explaining that sometimes Jesus just reaches down to someone and blesses him for no reason at all.

The Lord says, "Here—take that!" And as Dr. Hill said those

words, he grabbed a book from the stack and threw it out into the audience. Then he said, "Or *you*—take that!" And he tossed out another volume.

At the bottom of the stack there happened to be a very fine Ryrie Study Bible. Dr. George Sweeting, then president of Moody, sprinted forward and rescued the Ryrie Bible before it could become the next blessing.

Twelve memorable points.

The next year, Dr. Hill returned to speak at the same conference. The very first words he said were, "Number thirteen!"

He was still preaching that same sermon.

It's true. Once you begin to talk about what you have if you have Jesus, prepare yourself for one long discussion. You could talk about it forever. And you could use Romans 5 as a jumping-off point. All the riches are cataloged here. First, however, you need to step back and realize the emotional range Paul has brought to this conversation.

The first chapter of Romans is downright terrifying: a widescreen documentary of the wickedness of the world.

The second chapter covers anyone left out by the first—that is, the "non-wicked" (at least any claimants to such). The religious elite have no excuse, Paul announces.

If the Pharisees stood and applauded during the first chapter, then sat in shocked silence during the second, Paul may well have been speaking to an empty room by chapter 5. That would be unfortunate, because there is a seismic shift in the change of tone here. Paul now delivers the most thrilling news in the history of the world.

It makes sense. The happy ending of a classic story is only powerful when the hero has struggled with deadly enemies. In Newton's terminology, our hearts must be taught to fear before those fears can be relieved. In the initial chapters of Romans, Paul has dimmed the spotlight and told a tale of fear until its blackness and bleakness became unbearable. The most terrible thing about this horror story is that we ourselves are the characters within it. Now Paul brings up the lights and tells the part of the story that we've been longing to hear—though it is far more wonderful, far more gratifying than our feeble imaginations could have painted it.

THE SEVEN WONDERS OF GRACE

Think of the opening of Romans as Paul's tale of a traveler, a treasure seeker. This adventurer has struggled down a dark road filled with misadventure. Through all his fighting and struggling he has become a guilty man. Every crime alluded to by Paul can be laid at the feet of this seeker. He has been caught in a vicious cycle of evil from which there would seem to be no escape.

The adventure was never supposed to go this way. When he first set out, the traveler thought of himself as a champion. He believed he could overcome any obstacle and defeat any enemy. Now he stands in humiliation and close to the point of defeat. He hears behind him the rustling of the enemy, drawing closer and closer. The enemy is Death itself, coming to serve its writ of execution for the many crimes of this fugitive. The traveler grows weaker and weaker as he tries to flee; his arms and legs become entangled in the jungle vines, and quicksand is everywhere.

The traveler knows he lacks the strength to keep running, to keep fighting, to keep raising himself from every pit. He is willing to surrender to his relentless, pursuing enemy.

Then, just before giving up, the despairing traveler comes across a startling sight. There is a sudden clearing, cut perfectly through the trees and the bush and the vines. The clearing seems like a long row until he discovers another long row that bisects it. The clearing is cut in the shape of a great cross.

The seeker steps into the clearing and feels immediately safe. Death cannot enter a place of such light. And at the center of the cross, he finds a table with seven items upon it: the seven wonders of grace. After his long quest, he has discovered the riches of Christ's inheritance. These are the ancient treasures that every soul has been seeking since the beginning of time—even those who never realized the object of their quest.

These treasures are the inheritance of anyone and everyone who might claim them. Yet so few have done so. Turning to survey them, the traveler sees these things: a parchment, a key, a music box, a cocoon, a bottle, a map, and a trumpet. Surely each has a special meaning and a special purpose.

To find the solution to each puzzle, we must read Romans 5:1–11.

First Treasure: A Parchment

> *Therefore, having been justified by faith, we have peace*
> *with God through our Lord Jesus Christ.*
> —ROMANS 5:1

As the seven treasures are grouped, one is clearly set in front of the others. It is a parchment, rolled up and tied with a silk ribbon. As the traveler unrolls it and reads the text upon the document, he observes that this item is very old indeed.

The heading of the parchment reads: *Justified*—Declared Righteous. And just below this line, he finds his own name.

The holder of this document will hereby be absolved of all his guilt, absolutely and without exception. No past sin will be held against him. The Greek wording of this ancient document makes it clear that the traveler's justification is something that has already occurred—a completed action, a done deal! The seeker would judge that this parchment is some two thousand years old. But it is as durable and indestructible as eternity itself.

The ink is red. Only in the blood of God's own Son could such an order have been written and executed. When the Lord God issues a proclamation, it is irreversible. He does not change His mind. Can you imagine? The holder of such a proclamation need do nothing to earn or to maintain his or her innocence. It has been established and proclaimed once and for all.

Justification means that the war is over. Before the cross and before the love of Christ, we were the prisoners of our own self-destructive nature. There was nothing we could do to lift the charges of guilt that lay upon our heads.

The traveler feels an amazing sense of peace such as he has never felt. It begins to course through his whole being as he clutches the parchment to his chest. He realizes that his shoulders were stooped and weak from the invisible burden he had been carrying. Now the burden has fallen away, and his back feels young and strong again. *Peace*—a cease-fire in the holy war.

The fine print on the document reveals that this kind of peace is not about the easy life. On the contrary, the seeker knows there are many adventures and many exciting battles still to come. The peace is not a mere feeling but a state of reality. The word for it in Hebrew is *shalom*—the condition in which life can best be lived. This peace, according to the Jewish understanding, is salvation lived out right here on earth.

There is peace because the great enemy, Death, can no longer pursue him. He is at peace with God, free to walk in triumph rather than cower in fear. He is now God's servant rather than His prisoner. "And you, who once were alienated and enemies in your mind by wicked works, yet now He has reconciled in the body of His flesh through death" (Colossians 1:21–22).

This is the kind of peace Paul would describe again in another letter: "Be anxious for nothing, but in everything by prayer and supplication, with thanksgiving, let your requests be made known to God; and the peace of God, which surpasses all understanding, will guard your hearts and minds through Christ Jesus" (Philippians 4:6–7).

The traveler thrusts the document of peace into his shirt, where it will, as Paul says, guard his heart and mind in Christ Jesus. This treasure is the one that makes all the others possible. Without the parchment of justification, the traveler could never claim the other six that lie just beyond it.

Second Treasure: A Golden Key

> *Through whom also we have access by faith into this grace in which we stand.*
> —ROMANS 5:2

The traveler lifts a small golden key. Where is the door it unlocks?

As he holds it before him, he begins to *feel* the answer deep in his soul, and a startled gasp escapes his lips.

This is not the key to any earthly palace or storehouse. Through the cross, there is a new principle operating in his life and in ours. We now have free access to the grace of God—the same grace that has already declared us justified. It is as if the judge has signed the parchment and then invited us home with him rather than telling us to go on our way. The accuser is now a dear friend who wishes to share our company.

The word *access* is only used three times in the New Testament, and it always refers to the believer's access to God through Jesus Christ.

Grace is God's riches lavished upon those of us who, only moments before, stood accused. The prisoner on death row, of all people, has won the grand sweepstakes: the unsought, undeserved, and unconditional love of God. Like the traveler, we have been running through that jungle, always imagining the angry face of the Judge who will sentence us. We imagine Him to be in league with Death, our pursuer.

Yet it turns out that the Judge has been pursuing for love rather than vengeance. His face is compassionate rather than angry. And finally He pays the highest price imaginable so that He might provide that statement of justification that will allow restoration into His own family.

Once it has been accomplished, there is a new way to live. We have access to all the riches of grace. This key, in the hand of the traveler, represents the fact that the Father is saying, "Forget the past. All that I have is yours."

Grace must also be understood as a *standing*, just as Paul states it in Romans 5:2. It is a permanent condition rather than a sometime thing. As John Stott says, "We do not fall in and out of grace. . . . No, we stand in it, for that is the nature of grace. Nothing can separate us from God's love."[1]

Third Treasure: A Music Box

And rejoice in hope of the glory of God.
—ROMANS 5:2

As the traveler prepares to behold more of the seven wonders of grace, he reflects on the timeliness of these treasures:

The past: Justification for what we have done.
The present: Access to the glory of Christ.
The future: Promise of glory to come.

This third treasure is represented by a music box. Why such an odd choice for this wonder?

Paul is telling us that the promise of glory to come is a reason for celebration. It is like the father who throws a feast when the Prodigal returns. It is like John Newton deciding his emotions about grace can only find the right form in a triumphant hymn. It is Paul saying, "Rejoice in the Lord always. Again I will say, rejoice!" (Philippians 4:4). And is it even possible to rejoice without music slipping in?

Paul's word comes from the Greek *kaukaomia* which, interestingly enough, means to boast. This is not an in-your-face, braggadocio boasting but an uncontrolled jubilation. And we have permission to do this boasting, because it's all about God instead of us. We are celebrating a dream of the future that God has promised us will really come true. "But 'he who glories, let him glory in the Lord'" (2 Corinthians 10:17).

Oh, how much more often we would celebrate, and how jubilant our churches would be, if we paid more attention to the whispers of the future that lie on these biblical pages—whispers of hope about a glory that lies ahead. "To them God willed to make known what are the riches of the glory of this mystery among the Gentiles: which is Christ in you, the hope of glory" (Colossians 1:27).

Paul tells us, "When Christ who is our life appears, then you also will appear with Him in glory" (Colossians 3:4). The glory is in Christ alone, but we will share in its riches in an ultimate way. This will be the culmination of all our hopes and the joy to which our whole lives have pointed.

Have you noticed that the sweetest joys sometimes come in the anticipation of something? It's Christmas morning for a child, the wedding or future home for the young couple, even the simple anticipation of a hot bath when you're out shoveling snow in freezing temperatures. These are joys yet to come, and that sends a little shudder of pleasure through the frame.

It's like a music box that has the enticing melody of a far country, one that lies ahead. A music box is only a simple piece of machinery; it cannot suggest what the full orchestra can produce. But it is a reminder, and our imagination does the rest. This is a fine treasure indeed—a treasure that offers hope—and the traveler cherishes it.

Fourth Treasure: A Cocoon

And not only that, but we also glory in tribulations, knowing that tribulation produces perseverance; and perseverance, character; and character, hope.

—ROMANS 5:3–4

This next treasure is certainly the most curious yet. It is a cocoon!

The traveler wonders if it could really be a treasure at all. As he gently lifts it, he feels a slight tinge of pain in his hand. He knows immediately that this one is going to be quite different from the lovely music box. He looks more closely.

Paul has been telling us about glory. That's a terrific word. *Glory!* What could be more positive?

But here is Paul mixing it with *tribulations*. We don't like the sound of that. Isn't that the word that always goes around in the company of *trials*? Why would we "glory" in trials and tribulations? We're not gluttons for punishment. Where's the jubilation there?

The traveler has already realized that the peace received in the first treasure is no guarantee of an easy life. How could he have an adventure without a few dragons to slay? He lifts the cocoon again; and for the first time, as he gently squeezes it, he observes the miracle. An image of his face is there, like a reflection—but the reflection is changing.

As he applies light pressure, his face in the cocoon shows sadness. But the sadness begins changing into a kind of rugged strength: perseverance. That appearance, in turn, begins to show itself in a new, more admirable character in his features. As he looks even more closely at the image of his own face, he sees that it is taking on a powerful, confident look to it—a look of hope.

Like the odd little insect that becomes a butterfly, the child of God is constantly transforming into something more beautiful. It is the same process of development that Paul describes in these verses. The traveler remembers trying to slice his way through the jungle while only becoming weaker. Now, with this amazing treasure, he sees that the dragon's breath of fire can only make him stronger! Paul uses the Greek word *thlipsis* for "suffering," and the idea is a kind of pressure, as in squeezing grapes to extract the juice.

We don't go looking for trouble, but we certainly do make use of it. Bad times are our fuel for transformation. They make us stronger, nobler, wiser, and more worthy of serving God in ever-increasing capacity.

Take Paul, who gave us these words in Romans, through the inspiration of the Holy Spirit. Did he lead the life of luxury after he committed himself to God's service? Here is his own answer to that question:

> I speak as a fool—I am more: in labors more abundant, in stripes above measure, in prisons more frequently, in deaths often. From the Jews five times I received forty stripes minus one. Three times I was beaten with rods; once I was stoned; three times I was shipwrecked; a night and a day I have been in the deep; in journeys often, in perils of waters, in perils of robbers, in perils of my own countrymen, in perils of the Gentiles, in perils in the city, in perils in the wilderness, in perils in the sea, in perils among false brethren; in weariness and toil, in sleeplessness often, in hunger and thirst, in fastings often, in cold and nakedness—besides the other things, what comes upon me daily: my deep concern for all the churches. (2 Corinthians 11:23–28)

Now read Paul's letters—most of them written during and after all of these trials—and then answer this question. Has he become more positive or more discouraged? Is he wiser or more bitter? What has been the result of his constant tribulations? He sits in cramped prison cells awaiting his own execution and writes letters of joy and jubilation. For him, to live is Christ; to die is gain (Philippians 1:21). It's a win-win proposition when you understand your life as a cocoon.

Paul has come to realize that no matter how hard you squeeze him, all you can do is help the process along—the process of transforming him to the image of Christ. There is nothing the world can throw at us that God will not use for His glory and our eternal joy.

The traveler cradles the cocoon gently in his hands. He begins to realize that this treasure is every bit as precious, every bit as essential as those that came before it. He looks carefully into the little chamber of transformation again and begins to understand the process in three steps.

1. *From tribulation to perseverance.* It's the idea of tempering steel. The flames only make the iron stronger. Suffering without the hope of Christ leads to defeat and bitterness, but through the wonders of grace, we develop perseverance through our trials. We take the blow; and the next time it comes, we face it more squarely.

As the prophet phrased it, "I will bring the one-third through the fire, will refine them as silver is refined, and test them as gold is tested. They will call on My name, and I will answer them. I will say, 'This is My people'; and each one will say, 'The LORD is my God'" (Zechariah 13:9). Our suffering bonds us even closer with God.

John writes of these trials of faith in Revelation. Peter speaks of how intense heat purifies gold by burning away the dross. Jesus tells us in the Sermon on the Mount that we are blessed when we are persecuted. And Job, whose name is synonymous with suffering, says, "When He has tested me, I shall come forth as gold" (Job 23:10).

Do you catch the theme? Persevere, and your destiny is golden.

2. *From perseverance to character.* What exactly is character? Paul is referring to the idea of a character without impurities—a man or woman of integrity. James refers to this as the process of perfection: "My brethren, count it all joy when you fall into various trials, knowing that the testing of your faith produces patience. But let patience have its perfect work, that you may be perfect and complete, lacking nothing" (James 1:2–4).

When we endure, we begin to lose our fear. We develop the assurance of our own strength, knowing that the trial will not consume us. Such confidence gives us the character to act based on principles rather than out of desperation.

3. *From character to hope.* People of character are positive people. They live by the rules of righteousness, and they know it works. That positive pattern breeds hope and destroys the cynicism that is the mark of our age. How many truly hopeful people do you know? Hope springs from character, character from perseverance, and perseverance from tribulation—but only when we trust God to lead us through the fire.

Later in Romans, Paul writes, "For I consider that the sufferings of this present time are not worthy to be compared with the glory which shall be revealed in us" (Romans 8:18). Those are the words of a hopeful man. He is saying, "Do I have problems? Absolutely. But they're not worth talking about when we could be discussing the incredible things God has in store for us."

Read through your Bible for case study after case study. It is a book of godly men and women enduring the suffering that brought them godliness.

Lloyd John Ogilvie has written about the most difficult year of his life, a time when his wife underwent five major surgeries, radiation treatment, and chemotherapy, and when a host of other problems beset him all at the same time. He says, "Prayer was no longer a contemplative luxury, but the only way to survive. My own intercessions were multiplied by the prayers of others. Friendships were deepened as I was forced to allow people to assure me with the words I had preached for years. No day went by without a conversation, letter, or phone call giving me love and hope. The greatest discovery that I have made in the midst of all the difficulties is that I can have joy when I don't feel like it."[2]

We're all going to face problems. Wouldn't you rather face them as Dr. Ogilvie did, with an army of fellow believers and the counsel of the Holy Spirit encouraging you every step of the way? Don't you think joy makes a considerable difference? Yes, *joy*, in the midst of the worst that life has to offer. It all begins with the *knowledge* (Paul says "*knowing* that . . .") that life is not a cruel and random course of victimization. It is a cocoon: an orderly path toward the wonderful goal of being Christlike.

Fifth Treasure: A Bottle of Perfume

Now hope does not disappoint, because the love of God has been poured out in our hearts by the Holy Spirit who was given to us. For when we were still without strength, in due time Christ died for the ungodly. For scarcely for a righteous man will one die; yet perhaps for a good man someone would even dare to die. But God demonstrates His own love toward us, in that while we were still sinners, Christ died for us.

—ROMANS 5:5–8

The traveler is becoming more and more excited as he realizes the astounding worth of each new wonder. A small bottle now comes into his curious fingers. The label on the little bottle reads For Your Enrichment.

He carefully pulls out the stopper and curiously sniffs its contents.

Immediately, he feels as if he has stumbled into a dream of heaven. This is perfume, but not like any worldly cosmetic. As the traveler closes his eyes and concentrates on the rich aroma, what he feels is the fragrance of love captivating his whole being.

In these verses, Paul says that God's love has been poured out in our hearts by the Holy Spirit. He goes on to explain that this outpouring is particularly sweet and powerful because Christ died for the ungodly. This passage is John 3:16 expanded and expounded—Scripture's central message given its most vivid presentation.

Once the precious liquid in this bottle is poured upon the traveler's heart, the aroma will never become stale. The power is absolute and final: "Who shall separate us from the love of Christ? Shall tribulation, or distress, or persecution, or famine, or nakedness, or peril, or sword? . . . For I am persuaded that neither death nor life, nor angels nor principalities nor powers, nor things present nor things to come, nor height nor depth, nor any other created thing, shall be able to separate us from the love of God which is in Christ Jesus our Lord" (Romans 8:35, 38–39).

Real Christians have that essence about them. If you can't smell it on their breath, you can at least hear it in their words, feel it in their attitudes. The love of God seems to permeate their spirit, so that there is always enough love to spare. Who else could understand that the rude driver on the freeway probably just had a bad day? Who else could ask God to bless a completely intolerable boss? Who else walks into a room filled with quarreling church members and furthers peace through his or her very presence?

For these people, the love of God has become the supreme fact of life, because nothing can separate them from it. Nothing can take it away. It is greater and more potent than all the problems of the world, and it would wash these problems away like a springtime rain if enough of us were willing to let it happen through us.

Paul speaks of that love being poured out all over God's children, like a drink offering might have been poured on the altar in his time; like the blood of Christ flows over every one of our sins, washing them away forever. And we need to notice that it is the Holy Spirit who does this pouring, carefully directing every drop where it most needs to go.

Not that there is any careful rationing of those drops. The Lord God is not stingy. His love overflows us. It drenches us to the bone, to the heart. We will carry its aroma forever.

The traveler begins to pour the contents of the bottle upon his chest, hoping it will find his heart. He finds that no matter how long he pours, the sweet liquid just keeps coming. He can bathe freely in the abounding love of God.

Sixth Treasure: A Map

Much more then, having now been justified by His blood, we shall be saved from wrath through Him. For if when we were enemies we were reconciled to God through the death of His Son, much more, having been reconciled, we shall be saved by His life.

—ROMANS 5:9–10

The traveler finds another parchment, rolled up. Will it be a proclamation like the first one? No, he quickly discovers this one is a map. Everyone knows about treasure maps, but hasn't this seeker already found his treasure? Why would he need a map now?

The main idea behind these verses is that God has already achieved the more difficult task of dying for us when we were sinners. Why wouldn't He be able to perform the easier one, which is to live within us? Or as the early Christian John Chrysostom put it, "If God gave a great gift to enemies, will He give anything less to His friends?"

This is a map that works two ways. It shows the past and the future, and there is a great red cross in the very center that is marked You Are Here. He can see his own blackened sins quickly disappearing like invisible ink on one side. So much for the past. On the other side, beyond the red cross, his future steps are coming into focus. The details are not clear to him, but he sees that wherever he goes, that red cross will go with him to shelter and empower him.

Griffith Thomas writes, "If the death of Christ was the means of our reconciliation, the life of Christ will be the means of our preservation."[3]

This is not a map that tells us exactly where we will go; it is a promise that He will be our life and our Lord, that He will accompany us and empower us for every destination and every path.

The traveler realizes that in the center of the terrible jungle lies the cross that is a clearing, in the center of the clearing lie the treasures, and now in the center of his heart lies that cross; and wherever he goes, uncharted destinations or not, that cross will overshadow all, giving him the authority of Christ and His kingdom.

Seventh Treasure: A Trumpet

> *And not only that, but we also rejoice in God through our Lord Jesus Christ,*
> *through whom we have now received the reconciliation.*
> —ROMANS 5:11

And what is the final wonder? A trumpet, of course!

A what? "I'm not a musician!" mumbles the traveler. "I have no idea how to blow this thing."

Just the same, he knows these are no ordinary, run-of-the-mill ancient treasures. These are the treasures of our riches in Christ Jesus.

So the traveler shyly lifts the trumpet to his lips and lightly breathes into it.

A ringing call to arms issues from the bell of the trumpet. It is as if an angel did the trumpeting! What a happy, victorious song it is.

Paul says, "We also rejoice." And it's just about as simple as that. This is the second treasure that has instructed us to rejoice, but this final one is all about joy. We once were lost and now are found. Our hearts were taught to fear, and now those fears are relieved. What can we do but rejoice? We sound the music, so that it is heard far and wide. When people hear that trumpet's call, and when they see us rejoicing, they, too, will yearn for these treasures. And they will find that everyone may share them. We will gather together and share the wealth that is the totality of our spiritual possessions in Christ. The deepest joy of all comes when we share the joy and introduce it to seekers and travelers yet to come this way.

It is fitting, then, that the final treasure is a call to worship. What else could it be? I defy you to read Romans 5:1–11 slowly, thoughtfully, and prayerfully, as you meditate upon each of the seven wonders in your own life, without experiencing a renewed urge for worship and praise of Christ. His riches continue to shower upon us year by year, day by day, and moment by moment. I dare you to contemplate the power and love and goodness of the living God, to let His love flow over you today, and not feel a soul-deep joy, an all-encompassing peace, and a rising courage to face the challenges that this week brings to your life. And finally, I urge you to consider deeply whether you can accept this glorious wealth without sharing it with as many other human beings as you possibly can.

The jungle of this world, you see, is filled with desperate, weary people who have come to the end of themselves. Their hands and their feet are entangled in the coils of the world and all its sin. Their path is obstructed by the cultural darkness that seems to grow deeper with each passing day. And all the time, there is the sound of Death stalking the forest, drawing ever nearer. At the lowest rung of spiritual maturity, you might have compassion upon them and perhaps understand when they offend you. At the higher rungs, you will begin to reach out a hand of love.

Your friends, your acquaintances, perhaps even your family members are desperate for the peace you have found. The price has been paid for their sins to be forgiven and their names to be written in Christ's blood upon that timeless parchment. All they need is a messenger to tell them the glorious news.

Can you think of any good reason not to be that messenger?

Moments of Grace

Which of the seven wonders of grace do you most need right now? Close chapter 5 of this book and open chapter 5 of Romans. Read the first eleven verses aloud to yourself, slowly, thoughtfully, and prayerfully.

Using a small card, make a list of the seven blessings contained in these verses. Beside each entry draw a simple picture that illustrates that blessing. You might use the images suggested in *Captured by Grace*—a parchment, a key, a music box, and so on; or you might picture each blessing with a unique item from your own imagination. Then slip the card into your purse or pocket, having it available to intentionally share with someone in need this week. Show your list to that person, describe the symbols, and pass along the comforting provision of God's grace.

CHAPTER SIX

The Connecting Point *of* Grace

How Precious Did That Grace Appear the Hour I First Believed

J ohn Newton's life had become a living metaphor: life as a tempest. His days merged into one long voyage through turbulent waters, his ship pounded by storms approaching from any and every point of the compass. He was a man without a country, a vessel wandering with no port.

On this night, March 21, 1748, the young slave trader dozed fitfully in his bunk, uncertain whether it was sea or soul that propelled him from nightmare to nightmare. Finally, rising to clear his head, he became aware of a storm rocking the ship. All hands were awake, and voices were shouting with urgency. Water was beginning to flood the hold.

Newton wondered if this was how it all ended: entombed on the ocean floor—no Christian burial for one who had lived no Christian life. Sailor's instinct set in, and he rushed for the deck and air to breathe. Just then he felt a rough hand on his shoulder. "Bring me a knife," yelled the captain, shouting to be heard above the chaos.

Newton returned below to run the errand. As he did so, the man who took his place on deck was washed overboard. *That wave was meant for me*, thought Newton as he worked the pumps. He threw all his strength into the task and stammered, almost without thinking, "If this will not do, the Lord have mercy upon us!"

Mercy. That word leaped out at him as if some other voice had uttered it. *Mercy* wasn't typical of the words found in his vocabulary over these recent years. But what of that? What mercy, what compassion, what favor had anyone ever shown him? God had stolen his mother, and men had stolen everything else.

From three in the morning until noon the next day, when he was physically spent, Newton pumped water. He claimed one precious hour of sleep and then steered the ship until midnight. The job required a certain concentration, but Newton found it possible to let his mind wander for the first time in many hours. Long-suppressed thoughts and emotions spilled over his soul. He reflected over the tempest of an angry life.

As hope of survival began to take hold among the crew, Newton felt something happening within him. He couldn't explain it. He couldn't give logical reasons. He only felt a rising certainty that no mere accident of fate spared his ship. Something more than a random throw of the cosmic dice had allowed him to see another day. For the first time since childhood, Newton could actually *feel* a purpose to the fabric of the universe.

But the Agent of that purpose remained mysterious to him. God was a mysterious benefactor whose acquaintance he had yet to make.

"I began to pray," he would recall in his later writings. "I could not utter the prayer of faith; I could not draw near to a reconciled God, and call him Father. . . . The comfortless principles of infidelity were deeply riveted. . . . The great question now was how to obtain faith."[1]

Newton continued to ponder these questions as his long watch on deck continued. When he was finally relieved at the wheel, he hurried to the supply cabin in search of a Bible. Paging through it, squinting at the lines, trying to remember the verses beloved by his mother—he came in time to Luke 11:13: "If you then, being evil, know how to give good gifts to your children, how much more will your heavenly Father give the Holy Spirit to those who ask Him!"

It seemed as if the verse was placed there especially for his eyes. *If you then, being evil . . .*

If the book were true (and his blessed mother had staked everything upon it), then this verse must also be trustworthy. And that would be the most wonderful of all possible truths, for what it offered was *help right now.* "I have need of that very Spirit, by which the whole was written, in order to understand it aright," he would write. "He has engaged here to give that Spirit to those who ask: I must therefore pray for it; and, if it be of God, He will make good on His own word."[2]

Newton was hardly aware of the movements of his ship as it completed its voyage. He was deep in thought, lost in prayer, buried in Scripture. Three weeks later, the boat anchored in Ireland—and the storm returned with a fury the very next day. With a chill, Newton realized there would have been no survival if the ship had been a day later in docking. It was as if a heavenly hand had restrained the wrath of nature just long enough for his crew to harbor safely.

Newton would later say that he had embraced the truth of the Gospels and the power of their Savior to rescue him from the hell he had fashioned of his own life. There in the pages of Matthew, Mark, Luke, and John, he found the one and only hope that his soul could be rescued from the anguish and despair that had become his permanent dwelling place. It was hard for him to believe: all his sins, blotted out in one moment; all that was wretched about him, forgiven.

There was powerful emotion in this feeling of absolute mercy that was vast enough and generous enough even for his miserable soul. He felt an earnest yearning to repent of the sins he could identify and to live now for that Savior of mercy. He even smiled as he felt deliverance from the lesser matter of swearing, so common to sailors. He was excited to know that his tongue would now reflect the kingdom of God rather than the sordid places of the world.

Newton later believed that at this point, his conversion was not yet accomplished. In his own judgment, his soul was still in the grip of unacknowledged sin. He had the knowledge but not the acquaintance of the Christ of the Scriptures. As he would later describe it, "I had no apprehension of . . . the hidden life of a Christian, as it consists in communion with God by Jesus Christ; a continual dependence upon him."[3]

Looking back, he would feel that many miles and many trials still lay before the younger Newton before he would finally enter the secure embrace of His Savior. In the late autumn of his years, at the age of eighty, he would find himself writing in his diary upon the fifty-seventh anniversary of the storm that could have claimed him yet helped to deliver him: "March 21, 1805. Not well able to write. But I endeavor to observe the return of this day with Humiliation, Prayer, and Praise." This had become a personal day of remembrance. For over half a century now, he had marked the anniversary with thanksgiving and reverence.[4]

Seventeen centuries earlier, another old man sat with pen in hand, lost in his own memories. His eyes were failing, but there were sometimes young friends to assist him. He thanked the God of heaven for those friends. He wrote them frequently: teaching, encouraging, pleading occasionally for visits and assistance. He found that he couldn't discuss the journey of the Christian faith without recounting his own voyage. In many ways, his passage had paralleled that of John Newton. We know it by reading his letters.

Yet it would be a traveling companion named Luke who would tell the apostle Paul's story in its fullest version. His conversion is well documented, being detailed three separate times in the book of Acts. The story occupies more space in the New Testament than any other record except those surrounding the crucifixion of Christ.

Why is so much importance attached to the conversion of Paul? Griffith Thomas replies that the future of the Christian church pivoted upon this one event. A singular conversion experience for a singular individual: Paul was a Jew by birth, a Roman by citizenship, a Greek by education, and eventually a Christian by grace; a missionary, a theologian, and evangelist; a pastor, an administrator, a philosopher, and a statesman.[5]

SAUL THE HUNTER

Then Saul, still breathing threats and murder against the disciples of the Lord, went to the high priest and asked letters from him to the synagogues of Damascus, so that if he found any who were of the Way, whether men or women, he might bring them bound to Jerusalem.

—ACTS 9:1–2

The man we know as the apostle Paul, who transformed his world more than anyone other than his beloved Master, first appears as an ambiguous face in the crowd. Saul, as he was then known, is the witness to an episode of mob violence. He is a passive young observer at the martyrdom of an early Christian leader. Stephen is that leader: a man described as having an angelic face; a rising star among the Jesus followers, just as Saul is a rising star among the enemies of Jesus.

These are volatile days in Jerusalem, for the Christian church is newly born. It is Stephen who captures the ire of the religious status quo. Its enforcers pursue him out of Jerusalem and stone him to death, laying their cloaks at the feet of "a young man named Saul" (Acts 7:58). The year is most likely AD 35.

The next time Saul is mentioned, we notice the word "consenting," as opposed to simply observing. Saul finds himself endorsing the violence (Acts 8:1). He is a young rabbi, quickly learning his way beside his elders. Mob fever is a highly potent contagion. It reaches out to infect and demonize bystanders. We have seen this in the streets of Munich in the early 1930s, in Paris in 1789, and even in Los Angeles in 1992.

There is something restless and highly flammable inside Saul of Tarsus. He was passive, then approving, then at the head of the line attacking the young church. By Acts 8:3, he is dragging away believers to imprisonment.

Finally, in Acts 9:1, Luke uses the Greek word *phonos* to describe the work of Saul. The translation is "murder." "Then Saul, still breathing threats and murder against the disciples of the Lord . . ." The young Pharisee now has the blood of the martyrs on his hands. The persecution of the church has completely taken possession of his soul. Saul of Tarsus has found his calling.

Compared to the Pharisees we meet in the Gospels—more critical and cynical than explosive—Saul has become somewhat of a hit man of the holy mob. He is breaking into home meetings, participating in scourgings, and attacking men and women alike.

Finally, when the Jerusalem church lies in ruins, he finds that he has not sacrificed enough blood to the demanding gods within himself. The cravings of sin can never satisfy but only demand larger offerings. Saul appears before the high priest and asks for permission to take his show on the road. By this time, Christians have fled Jerusalem in terror, seeking refuge in cities such as Damascus, the capital of Syria. Christians there have established an outpost and are already proselytizing Jews in the local synagogues. In the back of his mind, perhaps Saul wonders why these heretics cannot keep their mouths shut when it places their lives in danger. In any case, he wants to hunt them down, get them in shackles, and deliver them to Hebrew justice in Jerusalem.

Listen to his own confession. Here he refers to the church as The Way, as it has begun to describe itself: "I persecuted this Way to the death, binding and delivering into prisons both men and women, as also the high priest bears me witness, and all the council of the elders, from whom I also received letters to the brethren, and went to Damascus to bring in chains even those who were there to Jerusalem to be punished" (Acts 22:4–5).

This Way has become a difficult road because of the tireless attacks of Saul, who is now striking from a distance. "Being exceedingly enraged against them," he will later recall, "I persecuted them even to foreign cities" (Acts 26:11). He will describe himself as "a blasphemer, a persecutor, and an insolent man" (1 Timothy 1:13). Much like John Newton, he will struggle to find words to express the abhorrence he feels for his early life. He will view himself as the chief of all sinners (1 Timothy 1:15).

Self-righteous anger always feeds on some hidden fire. Something inside Saul made him unrelenting in the bloodiness of his attacks. He could have murdered every Christian alive and started on other sects and cults, and still the burning would have endured. Maybe he had a dawning realization of that fact in time and began to realize that some greater Power was trying to speak to him.

One way or the other, violent emotions can only be ratcheted so high. Sooner or later there would have to be a reckoning, not with the enemy in Damascus but with the true demon that lay within himself.

SAUL THE HUNTED

From the beginning of our faith, converted Christians have spoken of God not as a passive deity hiding in His throne room but as a relentless pursuer—a heavenly Shepherd gathering in every single lost sheep. The most compelling word picture may come from a poet named Francis Thompson.

Thompson was a homeless man on the streets of London, often earning a few pennies by selling matches. So ashamed was he that when he sent a few poems to a magazine, he would give only the return address of a chemist's shop. The editors, startled by the quality of the poetry, sought him there and found that place to be where Thompson fed his opium addiction.

Thompson went on to write a poem called "The Hound of Heaven," about the God who follows us until we become His own. The poem begins this way:

I fled Him, down the nights and down the days;
I fled Him, down the arches of the years;
I fled Him, down the labyrinthine ways
Of my own mind; and in the mist of tears . . .

From those strong Feet that followed,
followed after,
But with unhurrying chase,
And unperturbed pace,
Deliberate speed, majestic instancy,
They beat—and a Voice beat
More instant than the Feet—
"All things betray thee, who betrayest Me."

Finally, after fleeing and hiding in every possible false refuge,

Halts by me that footfall:
Is my gloom, after all,
Shade of His hand, outstreched caressingly?
"Ah, fondest, blindest, weakest,
I am He Whom thou seekest!"

Men and women who do the pursuing can only capture empty air. Nothing satisfies. This indeed is the definition of religion. What sets apart our Christian faith is the story told in reverse—one of a loving Father who pursues *us* because we are too foolish and too sin-stained to go to Him.

Read the thoughts of all the great people of faith through the ages, and you'll find that common denominator. God pursued them "down the nights and down the days." For example, C. S. Lewis writes, "I never had the experience of looking for God. It was the other way round: He was the hunter (or so it seemed to me) and I was the deer. He stalked me . . . took unerring aim, and fired. And I am very thankful that this is how the first (conscious) meeting occurred. It forearms one against subsequent fears that the whole thing was only wish fulfillment. Something one didn't wish for can hardly be that."[6]

Saul saw himself as the relentless hunter. Yet he must have begun to realize that he had become the hunted. "All things betray thee, who betrayest Me." Naturally the divine encounter finally occurred just where a tale of pursuit should: on a road.

Confrontation

What were the thoughts of Saul the merciless as his entourage traveled the Damascus Road? Perhaps he was imagining the violent scene that lay before him in a few hours. Perhaps he was savoring the anticipation of another city cleansed from the Christian disease.

But maybe not. Could it be that by now Saul was at war within himself? We can't know his precise thoughts when "As he journeyed he came near Damascus, and suddenly a light shone around him from heaven" (Acts 9:3).

The apostle will later tell this story and fill in several details. For instance, the event transpired at high noon (Acts 22:6; 26:13). We are assured it was no natural phenomenon, no heat-related stroke or hallucination, for the invading light was more brilliant than the noonday sun.

We also learn that the event was experienced by all of Saul's companions, but only Saul understood the voice that everyone heard. The others "stood speechless," recognizing the presence of a supernatural phenomenon but not understanding it (Acts 9:7).

Finally, we learn that it was Jesus Christ himself who met Saul along the road. It was His voice that spoke the words that would haunt the young man for the rest of his life.

Ever since that day, commentators have looked for a psychological or natural explanation for this idea of Jesus appearing to Saul. Maybe he fabricated the entire incident later as counterfeit credentials for his insistence upon apostleship.

These rationalizations simply don't square with any piece of evidence that we have. Saul saw Christ, and his traveling companions saw and heard *something*. Then the Lord spoke of it independently to a man named Ananias, who didn't even know Saul, except through his infamous reputation. We could no more credibly explain the event as "mass hallucination" than we could the Resurrection. History makes its case clearly. The best evidence of this miracle's authenticity is the undeniable effect it had on Saul—just as the best evidence for the Resurrection is what happened to those disciples who witnessed the supernatural power of God and were transformed instantaneously.

Paul holds the status of an apostle because he saw the risen Lord. He writes, "Am I not an apostle? Am I not free? Have I not seen Jesus Christ our Lord? Are you not my work in the Lord?" (1 Corinthians 9:1). The early church accepted his experience as a valid one and counted him the equal of Peter, James, John, and the rest.

As far as the revelation of Scripture is concerned, this was the first appearance of Christ since the martyrdom of Stephen. Christ has brought things full circle, appearing to an assassinated Christian leader and then to one of the killers—who in godly irony would succeed him.

Conviction

The words Christ spoke to Saul are serious and direct: "Then he fell to the ground, and heard a voice saying to him, 'Saul, Saul, why are you persecuting Me?' " (Acts 9:4).

These would be the words of a judge or a prosecuting attorney—except that their context is unmistakably personal. Saul's name is called twice, as if painfully: "Saul, Saul!" Then, "why are you persecuting Me?"

Saul might never have given a thought to whom he was persecuting, other than Jewish heretics, who, in his view, were spiritual blasphemers who threatened the venerable faith. He never considered that he would find himself kneeling in the dust before these disciples' Master.

In Saul's mind, he had been reforming. He had been cleansing. He had been investigating and arresting, and yes, applying sanctions: prison or physical torture. He had just been doing his job, giving it 100 percent. Nothing personal!

Until now.

The voice he hears is Aramaic, the authentic language of his fore-fathers—the language spoken, in fact, by Jesus. "Saul, Saul, why are you persecuting Me? It is hard for you to kick against the goads" (Acts 26:14).

Saul the zealous rabbi, blinded by an almost radioactive light, struggles with two new and shocking facts:

First, he is speaking to Jesus, who is *not dead.*

Second, Saul has been attacking Jesus himself and not simply His faceless followers.

Could it be that when we attack our fellow Christians in any way, by words or by church politics, we are attacking Jesus, who stands behind them and who is more alive and more present than we acknowledge? Could it be that what we dismiss as "fussing and feuding" in the church is not so harmless after all, because it drives yet more nails into those blessed wrists?

F. B. Meyer points out that in one agonizing moment Saul no longer sees himself as God's champion but as God's enemy. "By every blow he struck at the infant church, he was lacerating those hands and piercing that side. By every sigh and groan extorted from the members of the Body he had elicited from the Head in heaven the remonstrance, 'Saul! Saul! Why persecutest thou Me?'"[7]

Conversion

Saul's entire conception of God has been undermined in one fell swoop. Imagine discovering that the God you worship is Someone else entirely, Someone who bears radical differences to your most precious assumptions about Him. You would ask the very question Paul now asks: "And he said, 'Who are You, Lord?' Then the Lord said, 'I am Jesus, whom you are persecuting. It is hard for you to kick against the goads'" (Acts 9:5).

Saul knows the answer to his own question—he just hasn't had the time to process the vast implications. *Who are You, Lord?* The answer to that question will force a new one: *Who am I?*

Just when Saul thought he knew all the answers, the questions have changed. What does he do with his deep reserves of anger? It all becomes fear, in one terrible instant.

It is hard for you to kick against the goads. Everyone in Saul's world knows about the ox driver and his long pole, the end of which carries a sharpened piece of iron. That point "goads" the ox to move where he is instructed. But the constant jabbing is painful, and every farmer knows there are times when the ox will turn on the goad stick and attack it—which of course only increases the pain.

For the ox known as Saul, what are the goads? Christ is saying that something has been pricking away at Saul, trying to guide him to proper plowing, but he has been bloodying himself by resisting.

The goading may have begun with the words that came from the mouth of Stephen, who accepted his cruel death with amazing grace. Stephen's face shined "as the face of an angel" (Acts 6:15). Perhaps Saul felt something tugging at his heart, and he pushed back.

Next, it may have been the behavior of the Christian believers who prayed for Saul even as he attacked their families. It may have been the persistence of the people of The Way who would leave all that they had in Jerusalem to keep following Christ elsewhere—and then would dangerously reveal their position by telling everyone within earshot about Jesus.

Saul was not getting the point—he was slamming his head against it. *All things betray thee, who betrayest Me.* The Hound of

Heaven has drawn nearer and nearer in His pursuit, finally cornering him at high noon on the highway.

Consecration

Saul's first question has been, "Who are You, Lord?"

His second is the inevitable sequel: "So he, trembling and astonished, said, 'Lord, what do You want me to do?' Then the Lord said to him, 'Arise and go into the city, and you will be told what you must do.' And the men who journeyed with him stood speechless, hearing a voice but seeing no one. Then Saul arose from the ground, and when his eyes were opened he saw no one. But they led him by the hand and brought him into Damascus" (Acts 9:6–8).

Saul's companions may be more fearful even than Saul. At least he can understand what is being said to him. For their part, they see a light, hear a voice, and discover that their leader, so reckless and aggressive only moments ago, is now blind, trembling, and helpless. He has led believers to their prison; now he must be led by hand to his deliverance. Saul experiences the ultimate humility that physical helplessness always brings. He has depended only upon himself, but now he must learn to depend on the kindness of strangers.

Communion

Now comes the true agony. Saul must be left to deal with himself in a lightless world. "And he was three days without sight, and neither ate nor drank" (Acts 9:9).

These three days must have been the longest of Saul's life. What does a man do for three days in utter darkness, after his very identity and his convictions have been violently stripped away from him?

If he is a weak man, he flees into denial. He ignores his senses. Perhaps he even loses his mind.

But if he is a strong man—and Saul is one—he thinks. He processes. He tries to reconceptualize reality in the light of recent evidence.

There is so much to reconsider and relabel. We can imagine that his past life and career flash before him, as if they were the life and career of someone else entirely—some very evil person, drawing pleasure from the way he has destroyed lives, taking part in murder and torture, looking to new cities to persecute adherents of the Christian faith.

Even while blind, he sees more clearly than ever before. Perhaps in his dark world, that angelic countenance of Stephen looms again before him—a follower of this truly living Christ whom Saul has helped to destroy, even if passively. He sees face after face, sometimes of women and children, all people he has attacked without any provocation other than a difference in spiritual paradigms. And he wonders—what of his own spiritual paradigm now? How will these eruptions change him?

For three days, he refuses food or water. For three days, he faces the violence of his revelation squarely, without distraction, without subterfuge. This is simply the character of Saul, and surely one reason that God chose him. Saul is a man of powerful integrity and resolve. If he believes in the way of the Law, he will pursue it with all his strength. If he discovers that Jesus is real, he will face that truth with all his concentration and follow every implication to the action it demands. He is not given to half-measures.

The voice of Christ has said, "Why are you persecuting Me?" The voice has said his name twice, with emotion. The Man behind the voice has knocked him in the dirt and blinded him and left him among strangers. Why didn't this Lord of power kill him on the spot? Why has He brought him to this place?

Then Saul begins to see the faces again—Stephen and the rest of them. There is love in those faces. It is not like the serious, stodgy, often angry demeanor of Saul's own brand of faith. No, there is compassion, forgiveness, mercy—the true word for it would have to be *grace.*

Saul has impatiently listened to some facts about the Nazarene and His teaching. They are distortions of the words of Jesus for the most part, but still Saul can tell that the Lord was not one to call for violence or retribution. He was a man of grace. This must be why He did not knock the Pharisee from his horse and then finish him off. This is why the Lord obviously has the power to deal with *all* His persecutors, yet doesn't.

Grace—that must be the key to the whole enigma. Grace, a subject that might as well be foreign language to the Pharisees.

Saul saw Ananias in a vision. He heard the man's voice when Ananias came and found Saul at the street called Straight. Saul must have almost laughed, for this fellow was quaking with fear of the notorious Hebrew hunter. Yet Ananias trusted his Jesus so much that he obediently came in search of the one he always prayed wouldn't come in search of *him.* And there was a gentleness about Ananias as he laid his healing hands upon Saul of Tarsus. There was no anger or resentment, only *grace.*

All of these people, captured by grace.

Thirty years after the martyrdom of Stephen, the day will come when Paul bides his time in a Roman prison and awaits the same kind of fate as many of the people he once arrested. Perhaps he sees one more time the face of Stephen and of so many others since then, no longer enemies but brothers and sisters in the faith. By now he has lived and taught and served in the power of grace.

And he will face the executioner with no less love, no less compassion. He will go out with grace.

John Newton spent many hours thinking about that. He wrote a great deal about the life and career of the man who became better known as Paul. Newton always returned with fascination to the fact that God had selected the most terrible of His antagonists, not for special punishment but for special ministry.

A man like Newton, who had the blood of African slaves on his hands, could draw a lot of hope from a fact like that. He might have thought, *For God to pursue so seriously, so relentlessly, a child who has insulted His goodness in every way—there must be high purpose.*

C. S. Lewis, too, marveled at the Hound of Heaven, who never loses the scent:

> You must picture me alone in that room in Magdalen, night after night, feeling, whenever my mind lifted even for a second from my work, the steady, unrelenting approach of Him whom I so earnestly desired not to meet. That which I greatly feared had at last come upon me. In the Trinity Term of 1929, I gave in and admitted that God was God and knelt and prayed: perhaps that night, the most dejected and reluctant convert in all England. I did not then see what is now the most shining and obvious thing, the Divine humility which will accept a convert on even such terms. The prodigal son at least walked home on his own feet. But who can duly adore that Love which will open the high gates to a prodigal who is brought in kicking, struggling, resentful, and darting his eyes in every direction for a chance of escape? [8]

Do you think that Heavenly Pursuer is only after challenging game such as Paul, John Newton, or C. S. Lewis? I think you know better.

The love of Christ is on your trail, too, my friend. Even if you have already given in, "kicking, struggling, resentful" like Lewis, or "blindest, weakest" like Francis Thompson, He continues the pursuit. No, He does not wait impatiently for you to say the prayer of salvation and then turn on His heels to abandon you in favor of other sport. The truth is that the grand chase never ends—not until you totally resemble Him yourself. That is an eventuality none of us reaches in this life.

You can be certain there are parts of your identity, your hopes, and your dreams that are still on the run. You may harbor ambitions that need to be converted to godly ones. You may relate to your spouse or your parents or your coworkers in ways that Christ longs to bless with His love and grace, if you would only let Him.

What will it take? Being knocked down? Losing your sight? What must God do to captivate your attention and make you realize that He is alive, gloriously alive?

Perhaps you need several days of utterly focused fasting, such as Paul had, to work through the implication of His lordship on your personal world. Perhaps you need a long and thoughtful voyage by yourself, like Newton.

Even so, let the chase continue! We could have no more loving Pursuer. This is the story of your life: He will follow you until you follow Him. It will continue until your whole being has been captured by grace.

Moments of Grace

Perhaps the Hound of Heaven is pursuing you now. It's a love chase, as He seeks you for your own good. If this is true, how should you respond?

Think again of the startled words of Saul as Jesus appeared to him on the Damascus Road. Saul shouted two questions at the brilliant form whose glory had blinded his eyes and sent him reeling from his horse. Which of the two questions is most appropriate for you at this point in your life?

Who are You, Lord?
What do You want me to do?

Even if it takes several days of fasting and prayer, focus on those questions until Christ captures your heart with grace. If you've been a Christian many years, focus on that last question and reaffirm that you're doing what the Lord wants you to do, fulfilling the perfect will of the God of all grace.

PART TWO

GRACE
for the
PRESENT

CHAPTER SEVEN

The Confusing Paradox of Grace

Through Many Dangers, Toils, and Snares I Have Already Come

B y the time we get around to singing the third verse of John Newton's great hymn, we might be thinking several things:

Are we going to sing every single verse?
When is the part about being there ten thousand years? That's the coolest part.
These shoes aren't very comfortable.
I wonder if I could sing the alto part? I get tired of soprano sometimes.
Hmm, I wonder what these words are all about . . .

Every now and then, someone stumbles upon that last thought. What a nifty concept! You and I can actually pay attention to the words and ideas as they emerge from our lips. I've heard of Christians trying this and experiencing an immediate "worship upgrade," from business class to first class.

Sometimes I wonder what would happen if we slipped in some *different* lyrics one Sunday. Maybe we could sneak in a new verse to "Amazing Grace" that went:

> *I sing every hymn each week in church,*
> *I make every note sublime,*
> *I never pay attention to a single word,*
> *I'm thinking of dinnertime.*

Wouldn't it be fun to look out at the congregation and count how many singers noticed the change and how many just went on harmonizing?

That one is a verse you'll probably never sing, but I would venture that you've sung the following one:

> *Through many dangers, toils, and snares I have already come.*

As you sing those words, what do you usually think about? Do you reflect upon the dangers, toils, and snares through which you have already personally come?

John Newton didn't write those words because they sounded good or to give the organist an opportunity to play some effective minor chords. He wrote them because he had lived them. It's remarkable how many close encounters with death this man had. I visualize his office as having a file cabinet with three drawers: the top one labeled Dangers, the middle one Toils, and the bottom one Snares—all packed with files.

Consider a few of his highlights:

- At a shooting party, Newton almost killed himself by accidentally firing his shotgun while scrambling up a bank. The bullet singed the edge of his cap, missing his head by a couple of inches.
- During the storm described earlier, he was sent below deck while the man who took his place was washed overboard.
- Similarly, at the last minute, his captain oddly pulled him away from a river trip in Africa. That boat sank; and once again, the man who took his place drowned.
- Newton once tried to go overboard and retrieve his fallen hat. He was so intoxicated at the time that he nearly drowned. Even sober, he couldn't swim. Someone grabbed him and pulled him back.

Brushes with death have a way of making us consider great big questions about life and eternity. Newton's own close calls edged him closer and closer to his conversion experience. He regarded his survival as proof of the hand of Providence sustaining him over and over, when by any human reckoning he should have perished. Salvation meant more than the hope of heaven to him; it was a literal experience that he had many times, and the sum total of it persuaded him that God must have a particular purpose for his life.

Wouldn't you love to be in heaven when John Newton and Paul sit together and exchange war stories? Believe it or not, you would notice that Paul's were even more hair-raising than Newton's. And Paul's days of pursuing Christians were almost dull compared to his life *after* he became a believer. The book of Acts can be read as a kind of Spirit-filled James Bond movie from the first century. The apostle faces death every chapter or two, then he dusts himself off and proceeds to the next calamity.

Here are a few of Paul's action scenes:

- He survived a murder plot by the Jews first and then the Greeks (Acts 9:23, 29).
- He was stoned nearly to death then dragged out of a city. Left for dead, he later got on his feet and walked to a new city (Acts 14:5, 19–20).
- Having managed to get the entire city of Jerusalem in an uproar, he was dragged bodily from the temple and then pursued by Roman soldiers (Acts 21:30–32).

Even if John Newton talked about shipwrecks, Paul could say, "Been there, done that"—*three* of those, actually. He could talk about arguing the case for his life before rulers. He could tell about being lowered in a basket from an opening in the wall, to escape murder.

Perhaps it seems to you that your own life is fairly humdrum, not exactly Hollywood blockbuster material. You can imagine Paul and Newton looking up at you from that heavenly table and saying, "Now, what's *your* story?" And you'd begin to stammer, "Well, you see, I haven't had too many adventures really; I was a tax accountant" or, "I took care of the house."

But wait a minute. Think a little harder. We all have our portion of dangers, toils, and snares—dramatic or less dramatic, it really makes no difference. Have you ever lost a loved one and thought your heart would break? Have you experienced a painful divorce? Have you ever been out of work, unable to pay bills, and not certain what you were going to do in the immediate future? Or how about this one: have you ever been a parent? If the answer to that one question alone is yes, then you are an authority on dangers, toils, and snares. I know of no parent who hasn't lain awake nights worrying about his or her children for all kinds of reasons.

Trouble is like home. You're either there, coming from it, or on your way back to it. And I'm certain you've had your share of each of these:

Times of *danger* when you've been truly afraid.

Times of *toil* when you labored almost beyond endurance.

Times of *snare* when you've wrestled with temptation—sometimes winning, sometimes losing.

At this point, I'd like to suggest that you stop, put this book down for a few moments, and do some focused thinking. I urge you to make a list of your most important examples from each of Newton's categories.

Your Dangers:

Your Toils:

Your Snares:

Have you made your list? I'm serious about this. We're not in any hurry here. Let's go no further until you've thought carefully about your dangers, toils, and snares.

Got your list in hand? Good. You've reflected deeply at that pressure point where truth meets experience. Now you're in the right frame of mind to experience a blessing, because in the next few pages, Paul is going to offer us a theology of hope in times of crisis. If you can hold those personal experiences of yours with one hand and take hold of the Bible's guidance with the other, you'll undergo not only a worship upgrade but an everything-in-life upgrade.

One word of warning: if you get into the habit of *thinking* about these words rather than simply reading them, your life may be in significant danger of being changed for the better!

THE REQUIREMENT OF GRACE
FOR THE CHRISTIAN LIFE

But we have this treasure in earthen vessels, that the excellence of the power may be of
God and not of us. We are hard-pressed on every side, yet not crushed; we are perplexed,
but not in despair; persecuted, but not forsaken; struck down, but not destroyed.

—2 CORINTHIANS 4:7–9

Imagine a business traveler who is constantly on the go from one city to another, his appointment calendar packed. His clients always have some new crisis that he is expected to handle personally. It's one petty squabble after another, and he's always laboring to make peace between petty factions. His business is thriving, but there are plenty of headaches and no time for rest.

That was life two thousand years ago—at least for the apostle Paul. His business was church planting, and every new church brought new joy and new crises. Since Paul was the founder of so many congregations, he found himself in the middle of one controversy after another. Corinth was a problem church. There always seemed to be disruptions there: public immorality, divisions, and now a problem with false prophets. Some of them were challenging Paul's authority, and he wrote the letter that we know as 2 Corinthians to defend his credentials and to help the church members think spiritually about the problems they were encountering.

In 2 Corinthians 4:7, we find Paul trying to help his readers see the glory of our heavenly Father in the dust of everyday experience. That's what makes the difference in this life: seeing things from God's perspective. Paul is showing that it can be done, because God has been revealed in human form through Jesus Christ, the ultimate treasure in an earthly vessel—flesh and blood. All the eternal and infinite glory of God shined through the humanity of His Son, who was fully human and yet fully divine. Jesus' enemies saw Him as just another man, but behind those eyes dwelt the one true God.

That's fine. But what does it have to do with your problems or those of the Corinthians? Here comes the part that should send a chill up your spine, as it does mine. If we are ministers of Christ—and I don't mean paid ministers of a church, but the kind of minister every single Christian is by appointment—then we share in that eternal glory. As the Father dwelt in the Son, the Son dwells within us through the Spirit. We have this treasure, the ministry of Christ, in our "earthly vessels," our frail and imperfect human bodies.

This is a difficult concept to understand, but Paul always has a handy word picture available. This time he uses the idea of a clay jar. If there was one absolutely ordinary, run-of-the-mill object that everyone in the Middle East could understand, it was a clay jar. Cheap pottery was everywhere and used for everything. The jars were breakable, but it didn't matter because it was so easy to get another one. Clay earthenware was as common as—well, as the clay beneath one's feet.

A clay pot had absolutely no value in itself. Everyone knew that. On the other hand, it could hold a priceless pearl, a gold piece, a bite of bread to fend off hunger, a day's drink of water, a wedding ring, even a sleeping newborn baby. It wasn't the jar but the treasure inside that counted.

I know people who carry Bibles that look as if they've been through several shipwrecks with Newton. The covers are wrinkled and torn. The pages are nearly falling out. But the worn-out container holds the eternal Word of God.

It's not the vessel but its contents. A lowly clam hides a pearl; a lump of coal compresses into a diamond. We fall for one of the devil's greatest lies when we assume that our human limitations make any difference to the workings of God through us.

There will certainly be problems. Clay has its cracks, its heat limit, its fragility. But it still does the job and holds its precious cargo. "Just think about all that I've gone through," Paul is saying. "Is God any less real because I've been beaten and had rocks thrown at me? No—*more* so to us, because He bears testimony through all these things."

Dangers, toils, and snares. They just come with the territory. Paul tells Timothy he might as well expect to be mistreated, because the godly in Christ Jesus are always persecuted (2 Timothy 3:12). And in 2 Corinthians 12:7, Paul mentions his "thorn in the flesh." That one makes for an interesting story.

THE RESOURCE OF GRACE
FOR THE CHRISTIAN LIFE

It happened that Paul was once raised to the heavens by God to see glories no man had ever previously beheld. For the Lord's purposes, this vision was necessary for Paul. On the other hand, so was an infirmity of some kind. Why? Because Paul's supernatural experience would tend to breed pride. It could ruin him for ministry. Therefore God allowed a "thorn," literally a stake driven into the flesh. And "a messenger of Satan" was allowed to "buffet" or beat him. In 2 Corinthians 12:7, Paul speaks in language descriptive but not precise. He doesn't tell the precise nature of the suffering he endured, but he does tell us all we need to know: trials are allowed by God to help us keep perspective and to enable us to grow spiritually.

And it's interesting, isn't it? The greater the Lord's plans for us, the more we generally need to be tried. The more critical an army's mission, the harder the army needs to be drilled. The more significant the lesson you're teaching your children, the more discipline you'll need to employ. We think it strange when James tells us to consider it joy to endure a trial (James 1:2–3), but in truth, nothing could make more sense.

If you're involved in tough times right now, congratulations! God loves you, and He has great things ahead for you. Sometimes His earthen vessels simply need to be heat-treated.

Paul says of his suffering, "Concerning this thing I pleaded with the Lord three times that it might depart from me. And He said to me, 'My grace is sufficient for you, for My strength is made perfect in weakness'" (2 Corinthians 12:8–9).

It's good advice to consider our sufferings a joy, but no one is very good at that. Even Paul asked God to take away his trouble—his "thorn"—three times. The result? God turned him down three times.

Question: Is there any such thing as an "unanswered prayer"? Or would it be wiser to call them "unwanted answers"?

Yes, there are times when God doesn't give us what we want. But in those cases, He speaks to us in ways that are just as valuable as the thing we prayed for. The question is whether we are listening. In the case of Paul, for example, God gives this answer to the prayer: "My grace is sufficient for you" (v. 9). There is very rich, very practical wisdom in that answer—much more than a blunt "no."

It's as if God is saying to us, "I will not take away the trial, but I will give you the power to endure it." Here's another way of putting it: "I won't give you what you want, but I'll give you what you need. If I took away the trial, you would grow no stronger—in fact, you would be just a little weaker and more helpless, like a pampered child. But if I allow the trial and help you endure it, you will be stronger, wiser, and more useful to Me."

Another long truth in God's short answer: there is power in the grace of God. The verb translated "is sufficient" is in the present tense—as is God's grace, which is always present. In every situation, we can rely on Him to provide strength and courage. He will never give us all that we want, but He will always give us all that we need.

Compare our Lord to the gods of all the world's religions and you'll find that grace is the difference maker. It is the x-factor that radically sets Him apart. Our God is "the God of all grace" (1 Peter 5:10). He is kind, benevolent, and longsuffering. We need not beg Him, bribe Him, or appease Him. He actually longs to bless us every single moment, every single day. He comes down to us rather than demanding that we climb the impossible ladder to infinity to reach Him. Grace is God taking the initiative.

In this same letter, Paul will explain, "God is able to make all grace abound toward you, that you, always having all sufficiency in all things, may have an abundance for every good work" (2 Corinthians 9:8).

Notice the repetition of the word *all*. *All* grace abounds toward us so that we are *all* sufficient in *all* things. He is all we need in all we face, so that for all we do, we can overflow with His grace and power. Did you know it was possible to live like that?

One Friday morning, British pastor Charles Haddon Spurgeon was challenging his ministerial students. He said:

> There are many passages of Scripture which you will never understand until some trying experience shall interpret them to you. The other evening I was riding home after a heavy day's work; I was wearied and depressed; and swiftly and suddenly as a lightning flash, this text laid hold on me: "My grace is sufficient for you!" When I got home, I looked it up in the original, and finally it dawned upon me what the text was saying, MY grace is sufficient for THEE. "Why," I said to myself, "I should think it is!" and I burst out laughing. It seemed to

make unbelief so absurd. It was as though some little fish, being very thirsty, was troubled about drinking the river dry; and Father River said; "Drink away, little fish, my stream is sufficient for you!" Or as if a little mouse in the granaries of Egypt, after seven years of plenty, feared lest it should die of famine, and Joseph said, "Cheer up, little mouse, my granaries are sufficient for you!" Again I imagined a man way up on the mountain saying to himself, "I fear I shall exhaust all the oxygen in the atmosphere." But the earth cries, "Breathe away, O man, and fill your lungs; my atmosphere is sufficient for you!" [1]

Think of it this way. When you have a big problem, ask yourself, "How big is the problem?" Then ask yourself, "How big is God?" I tremendously doubt the time will ever come when you find that the problem is the larger of the two. Kenneth Wuest says it this way:

There is enough grace in God's heart of love to save and keep saved for time and eternity, every sinner that ever has or ever will live, and then enough left over to save a million more universes full of sinners, were there such, and then some more. There is enough grace available to give every saint constant victory over sin, and then some more. There is enough grace to meet and cope with all the sorrows, heartaches, difficulties, temptations, testings, and trials of human existence, and more added to that. God's salvation is an oversize salvation. It is shock proof, stain proof, unbreakable, all-sufficient. It is equal to every emergency, for it flows from the heart of an infinite God freely bestowed and righteously given through the all-sufficient sacrifice of our Lord on the Cross. Salvation is all of grace. Trust God's grace. It is superabounding grace.[2]

The Results of Grace in the Christian Life

We agree that we are just ordinary clay pots to be used to display God's power. We even accept that we will be prodded by painful experiences in order to learn that grace provides all we need. Now the good news! Here's the upshot of our humbling and our thorns—the result of trials is strength.

The Grace of God Produces Power

> *And He said to me, "My grace is sufficient for you, for My strength is made perfect in weakness." Therefore most gladly I will rather boast in my infirmities, that the power of Christ may rest upon me. Therefore I take pleasure in infirmities, in reproaches, in needs, in persecutions, in distresses, for Christ's sake. For when I am weak, then I am strong.*
> —2 Corinthians 12:9–10

Paul hated the thorn that plagued him. But in time, he accepted it. He knew there could be no ministry if there were no trial, because this life wasn't about Paul's strength but God's. The weaker Paul appeared, the greater the Lord would be glorified. Let me ask you: if you were the most talented person in the world, would that help or hinder your witness? People would say, "You can believe what you want when you have that much natural ability." But when we see absolutely ordinary individuals change the world for Christ—and our history is absolutely filled with those—we can have no doubt of the presence of God in this world.

The next time you think it's all about your strength or talents, remember the following:

- God used an uneducated fisherman to be the church's first great leader. His name was Peter.

- God used a fix-it man sitting in jail to write *Pilgrim's Progress*, one of the greatest classics in the English language. His name was John Bunyan.
- God used a shy, obscure monk to set off the greatest Christian reformation in history. His name was Martin Luther.
- God used a Bible college dropout to preach the Gospel to more people than anyone in history. His name is Billy Graham.
- God used an ordinary shoe salesman to create revivals and new ministries all over the world. His name was Dwight L. Moody.

It was Moody who said, "If this world is going to be reached, I am convinced that it must be done by men and women of average talent." The story is told of an occasion when he was preaching in London. Members of the royal family and other VIPs were present. When Moody came to the name Eliseus in Luke 4:27 (KJV), he couldn't seem to get the word out of his mouth. He began reading the verse again from the beginning, but he still stammered over the *E* word. A third time: same results. Deeply troubled, he closed his Bible and said, "Oh, God, use this stammering tongue to preach Christ crucified to these people." From that moment he preached with a power his closest followers had never heard. The crowd was awed by the presence of God that evening.[3]

This is among the deepest of spiritual truths. Remember that the ultimate treasure in an earthly vessel is God's own Son, whom the establishment believed it could kill. Because He was composed of flesh and bone, they assumed He was simply one more man who could be squashed beneath the thumb of the Roman Empire. He was simply a peasant carpenter from Nazareth, or so they thought.

What if God had chosen instead to save the world as His chosen people wanted it saved, through the military genius of a fabulous leader? What would that say of God, if anything at all?

Instead, countless people have come to Christ through concluding that only one kind of power could possibly turn the world upside down as it did within decades. The weakness of humanity is the proper container to glorify God.

The Grace of God Provides Perspective

For our light affliction, which is but for a moment, is working for us a far more exceeding and eternal weight of glory, while we do not look at the things which are seen, but at the things which are not seen. For the things which are seen are temporary, but the things which are not seen are eternal.

—2 CORINTHIANS 4:17–18

When you struggle with some trial, your first question might be, "Why is this happening?" A better one would be, "What is God teaching me?"

It's difficult for us to remember that God's great desire is for us to see things as they really are, rather than as they appear to be. As Paul says, we see in a mirror dimly right now. He is always working to remove the fog so that we might share His heavenly perspective. Have you ever met a child who was given her every desire? What is the result of that kind of parenting? It creates spoiled, undisciplined children who believe the world will always serve their requests on a silver platter when they snap their fingers.

I'm sure you'll agree that good parents don't raise their children that way. Instead they deny their children certain demands when it is appropriate to do so. Effective parents are always using the moment for an object lesson. They let their children know that love is not the same as pampering. Would your Father in heaven be any less wise in His parenting? He refuses to solve all our problems, but He gives us all the sustaining grace we need for toughing it out.

Can you remember taking your child to a new Sunday school class when she was three years old? She may have cried. She may have clung to your legs and begged you not to desert her until the situation tugged at your heart. you may have experienced every impulse to simply give in and take your child to the adult class with you or stay with her in the child's class. You would have then failed to help your child learn how to adjust to a new environment. Instead, you would have taught her that a pathetic demeanor will manipulate desired results.

Now consider that time when you were in an adult-sized version of that situation: you were unemployed or grieving over a lost relationship, perhaps. As you cried out to God, don't you think it tugged at His loving heart? Don't you think He longed to gather you up in His arms and give you everything you wanted? But He loved you enough not to give in. He knew how much wiser and stronger you would become through learning to depend upon His grace in a time of storm. Once your pleading was over and you had calmed down— just as the child does in a new Sunday school classroom—you were able to hear God say entirely new things to you. You could feel yourself growing. You said, "I made it through this trial by trusting God, and next time I won't be knocked down so easily."

Let's consider the remarkable ways God nurtures us through our struggles, according to this passage of Scripture.

1. *Afflictions help us to anticipate glory.* Reigning with Christ requires suffering with Him—no cross, no crown. But holding the hand of Christ through the darkness gives us a glimpse of the glorious nature of deliverance that is to come.

2. *Light things help us appreciate heavy things.* Paul calls it "light affliction," and frankly, that's what most of our sufferings are. These are like smaller models of the "higher" suffering called death, and the higher glory of eternal life. God teaches powerful truth through lesser mediums.

3. *Temporary things help us appropriate eternal things.* "For the things which are seen are temporary, but the things which are not seen are eternal" (2 Corinthians 4:18). The hope of wearing Olympic gold drives athletes to persevere through, and even to value, the pain of dedication. Comparing the value of temporary pleasures with potential glory, they press on. Gold medals are of fleeting value. Some even turn up in pawn shops to be exchanged for a different metal. The goal before us also requires rigorous perseverance through pain. Unlike the hopeful competitor, we can have confidence that every trial, every struggle, has a particular purpose to produce in us some eternal value.

4. *Outward pain helps us accelerate inward progress.* "Therefore we do not lose heart. Even though our outward man is perishing, yet the inward man is being renewed day by day" (2 Corinthians 4:16). Isn't it exciting that modern-day science is only now beginning to affirm what the Bible has said all along? There is a close relationship between body, mind, and soul. This is why you've met people with physical challenges who have extra layers of wisdom that few others have attained. Bodily suffering drives us deeper. We find God at the broken places, teaching and encouraging.

John Newton wrote, "We will look back upon the experiences through which the Lord led us and be overwhelmed by adoration and love for Him! We will then see and acknowledge that mercy and goodness directed every step. We shall see that what we once mistakenly called afflictions and misfortune were in reality blessings without which we would not have grown in faith."[4]

We can't wish away our problems, and we're unlikely to put on a fake smile and pretend we're enjoying them. What we can do is meet them squarely and soberly, refusing to view them as random shots from an unkind world. Instead, we know they are necessary challenges for the positive growth we're intent on experiencing. Who wants to remain a child forever? We know we need a good workout. We know it's necessary to build our spiritual muscles. There are no muscles of any kind that strengthen without resistance.

When you're at the gym, sometimes you can get through a grueling cycle on some machine by thinking about the muscles that machine is helping. I suggest you do that very thing during times of struggle. Where can you "feel the burn"? What part of your character is going to be that much more godly tomorrow? My friend, perspective will completely change the way you approach challenges.

In one of his books, my friend Ron Mehl wrote these words: "Storms always leave us with a list of things to clean up and fix. They are times when God restores to us the things we lose through negligence, ignorance, rebellion, or sin. For the Christian, storms are a no-lose proposition. They help me to see and acknowledge the loose shutters, missing shingles, and rotten fence posts in my life while turning me back to the only One who can make the necessary repairs."[5]

The Grace of God Promotes Perseverance

We are hard-pressed on every side, yet not crushed; we are perplexed,
but not in despair; persecuted, but not forsaken; struck down, but not destroyed.
—2 CORINTHIANS 4:8–9

In 2 Corinthians 6:4–5, Paul lists his personal struggles as tribulations, needs, distresses, stripes, imprisonments, tumults, labors, sleeplessness, and fastings. Remember his authority was under attack at this church. Consider the fact that he chooses his *problems* as his credentials. Can you imagine a pastor offering such problems to a church as his résumé today? Paul would suggest sleeplessness and prison time as two of the reasons he would make a good pastor. And of course he would be right.

Notice also the four "gauges" Paul uses to demonstrate the difference the grace of God has made in his life (and will make in yours).
Each of these gauges takes some particular measure of the emotional
state. Imagine the first gauge. At one end of the gauge is the word
Victorious, at the other end, Defeated. Because of grace, the needle
keeps hovering near the victorious end of the meter, and that means
that in spite of the pressure, you can keep going. The second gauge
shows Confident and Despairing as the extremes, and, while we may
often be more perplexed than confident, because of grace, we are
never despairing. No need to slow down.

These gauges are the difference in an empty fuel tank and one
that is simply low. Grace makes that difference: you proceed with
caution, but you're not out of gas on the side of the road. Here are
the four gauges:

1. *He was pressured, but not defeated.* Paul is saying he feels the
pinch, but he isn't crushed. The term means being pushed into a nar-
row place. Paul was a man who spent time in some very small prison
cells. As you know if you've read his prison letters, his joy could not
be compacted by lack of space; it only became greater. Grace moved
that needle.

2. *He was perplexed, but not despairing.* Church problems left
Paul at his wit's end sometimes. But he never gave up, and he always
found the right answer. Grace kept him moving toward the right
solution.

3. *He was persecuted, but not deserted.* The word for "persecuted"
derives from the idea of being pursued or chased. As we've seen, Paul
knew something about that kind of hunting, and he also knew about
being hunted. Even when it seemed that his enemies vastly outnum-
bered his friends, he never felt deserted, because Almighty God was
always with him with sufficient grace for his every need.

4. *He was pounded, but not destroyed.* The verb here means "to be struck down." Paul was often knocked down but he was never knocked out. He was sometimes left for dead, but he did not die. He kept getting back up to preach the Gospel of God's grace. When he was in prison, his work seemed to flourish. To the very end of his life, he was planning on new destinations and new churches. The kind of hope Paul had cannot be suppressed no matter how you pound it. Grace renders it eternal.

The Grace of God Promotes Praise

Sometimes we can gather hidden jewels simply by taking a closer look at Paul's sentence structure.

For example, notice the three phrases in these passages that begin with the word *that.* It may seem to you like an insignificant word, but Paul actually uses it as a bridge from human action to godly destiny. *That* means "in order to" or "so that."

Here are the three statements:

2 Corinthians 4:7	*"that the excellence of the power may be of God and not of us"*
2 Corinthians 4:11	*"that the life of Jesus also may be manifested in our mortal flesh"*
2 Corinthians 12:9	*"that the power of Christ may rest upon me"*

Reading them together, we see a pattern emerge.
We do what we do:
- that *God's power* will be present in us.
- that *Jesus' life* may be manifest in us.
- that *Christ's power* may rest upon us.

Again, Paul is pointing us to a bridge that Christ has built. On this side of the river, you experience dangers, toils, and snares. It's so easy to be discouraged and to develop a negative and cynical attitude. Then our friend Paul beckons to us. He points to these bridges that seem to disappear into the fog that lies upon the river. We decide to cross those bridges, because things can't be any worse than they are on this side. On the other side, we find the limitless power of God and the rejuvenating life of Christ.

But what precisely are those bridges? They are *attitudes* about our lives and our trials. The attitudes of the world lead to a dead end. The attitude on these bridges takes us to a whole new world. We realize that there is a purpose to our pain. God is up to something, and it's always something very good, something worth cherishing hope for. We begin to trust, putting our eyes on Him rather than on our struggles. And having done that, we find ourselves walking— first one tentative step, then another. We hear the echo of our footsteps beneath the bridge. We move into that mist. And then we begin to make out the shapes that lie on the other side: shapes of maturity, of wisdom, of new strength and new service for God.

Before we know it, we're not thinking of our infirmities at all.

John Newton lost his wife on this side of the bridge. This was surely the ultimate test of his faith, for he had an abiding love for her after many years of marriage. Having been married for twenty-two years, he wrote her a letter that said, "Every room where you are not present looks unfurnished."[6]

But one day he began to face the prospect of living out his life in unfurnished rooms. He had hoped, with all of his heart, that he would precede his wife to the grave. But now it was clear that his beloved Mary was becoming weaker every day. Newton's friends worried about him; they couldn't imagine how he would handle life without Mary by his side.

The Christian should be "hard-pressed, yet not crushed; perplexed, but not in despair." Would Newton have that demanding level of spiritual maturity?

On the day of Mary's death, John Newton preached at the regular service time. The next day he visited parishioners, and finally he preached the sermon at her funeral. Did he grieve? Of course he did—powerfully. He would later write, "The Bank of England is too poor to compensate for such a loss as mine. But the Lord, the all-sufficient God, speaks, and it is done. Let those who know Him, and trust Him, be of good courage. He can give them strength according to their day. He can increase their strength as their trials increase . . . and what He can do He has promised that He will do."[7]

John Newton had tried that bridge and found it would bear his weight. As a matter of fact, the grace of God has limitless strength. Every single one of us can trust our very lives to it. It has never failed, and it never will.

His grace is sufficient, no matter what you may be facing right now. His grace will lead us through every trial imaginable, until we begin to look upon one another and see not ourselves but the image of Christ himself, our hope, our refuge, and our goal. On that day, you and I will look back upon these earthly anxieties with hearts of loving gratitude. Troubles are very real, but in the light of His shadow, they somehow fade into the mist.

Moments *of* Grace

Look back over the lists you made of your own dangers, toils, and snares. Are you beat up or upbeat? Are you drawing on His store-house of grace?

Your daily interaction with God's Word is a barometer of your capacity to access God's grace for each day's needs. Glance at your Bible for a moment. Does it show the wear and tear of heavy use, or does it appear to have just come out of the box? Are its verses under-lined and well marked? Have you claimed specific promises for spe-cific needs? What individual verses are you leaning on right now?

If you need to do better in this area and aren't sure where to turn, try reading through 2 Corinthians, the book in which Paul talks openly about his own struggles. This book contains many "victory verses." Find one or two, draw boxes around them in your Bible, and use them in claiming God's all-sufficient grace for your situation right now.

CHAPTER EIGHT

The Confident Promise of Grace

'Tis Grace Hath Brought Me Safe Thus Far,
and Grace Will Lead Me Home

There are times when we feel we've wrestled life into a shape that feels comfortable. We hope the time has come to reap some enjoyment from the daily pace. Life makes sense, and we feel a quiet sense of satisfaction.

In these times, we begin to savor those patterns of life that help us navigate the passage of time: the familiar arrival of the seasons, the rhythms of honest work and daily life, the subtle transitions of aging.

Then, like a thief in the night, some uninvited event breaks into our lives. In the flicker of a moment, the work of years comes undone. The dependable pattern is destroyed, and life as we know it seems to be threatened. Suddenly the world doesn't seem so orderly and natural but random and even heartless.

John Newton may have harbored a few of these reflections during the mid-1750s, when his own life was torn by crisis.

Everything had been going so well, right up to that afternoon in November 1754. On that day he was sitting at tea with his wife, enjoying the warmth of the drink and the fire in the hearth, chasing away the autumn chill. His mind happily moved among all the last-minute details of preparing for a new adventure at sea. In only two days, he would be the captain, piloting a brand-new ship on its maiden voyage—the *Bee.*

Seafaring men enjoy the anticipation of that next journey: assembling the crew, taking inventory, dipping pen in ink to inscribe that first entry in the ship's log. Surely Newton's mind was as busy as the bee that was his craft's namesake.

And then, just like that, his body toppled unconscious to the floor.

Mary screamed in panic. Her husband had passed out without warning. Only the regularity of his breathing showed any evidence of life. After that, he slowly woke to a terrible headache that would not depart, as well as a dizziness that would never do for a ship's captain. He was left no choice but to resign from the only career he knew. John Newton would never sail again.

His heart was broken as he followed the news of another man's appointment as captain of the *Bee.* As the ship vanished over the horizon, Newton felt he was watching his life's work fade with it. He could only settle into his own recuperation period and begin thinking about what to do with the rest of his life.

It wasn't long before more news arrived concerning the *Bee.* There had been a revolt onboard. The slaves had seized control, killing Newton's replacement, along with two other men.

What thoughts went through the retired captain's mind? *It could have been me. There but for the grace of God go I . . .*

Imagine yourself escaping death only through a strange and

sudden illness at the last moment. What would be your thoughts? How might it affect your outlook?

On the one hand, you'd surely be grateful that God had intervened to spare you. On the other, you might ask, "Lord, what plans do You have for me now? Sailing is all I know."

But more calamity was yet to come. Just as Newton was recovering from his attack, his wife fell into an illness of her own. For eleven months he cared for her, praying that God would not take her away—that in His providence He would spare the wife as He had spared the husband.

Doctors had to be paid. The cupboard had to be stocked. While Mary was still ill, Newton accepted a position as a tide surveyor in distant Liverpool. It was a good job, but one that required sacrifice. He had to leave his beloved Mary behind, in the care of others. At this point her survival was in question; the doctors had done all they could do. How agonizing to try learning the skills of a new trade while wondering if his soul mate still clung to life—or whether he would ever see her again.

God is good. Newton wept for joy and thanksgiving when the Lord healed his wife at the very threshold of death's door. It was a miracle! Now the couple could be together again. As they sat again by the fire, they puzzled over the mysteries of providence. Why had God called home another captain, yet, with the other hand, taken away Newton's career? Why had He so nearly called Mary home, only to relent at the last fateful instant?

It was a question of those patterns.

Viewed from one direction, it appeared that the pleasant patterns of life had been torn apart. Then one could turn the picture around and perceive there were other patterns at work—deeper ones, the complex workings of almighty God. His intervening hand was unmistakable. John and Mary agreed that the Lord worked in mysterious ways, His wonders to perform. He had His own timetables and His own purposes that formed an intricate web that no mortal could disentangle in this life.

The patterns of God were more mysterious than the depths of uncharted seas, yet His grace was clear as the driven snow. That grace was no mystery. It was absolute, all encompassing, as vast as the sky on a starry night above deck.

The conclusion of the matter was that life was strange, but God was good. John and Mary Newton must give Him their trust and harbor no anxieties about it. When Someone loves you, you count on Him.

The Foundation Stone of Romans 8:28

Newton's mind returned again and again to grapple with that profound sentence at the heart of the book of Romans, at the heart of God's Word, at the heart of God's character and every single person's life. Romans 8:28 is the foundation stone of the very workings of your destiny and mine. It is probably the most well-known line the apostle ever wrote—surely one of the most oft-quoted and memorized. Christians cling to it during the tempests of their lives like a wooden beam adrift in the sea.

Here it is, perhaps as familiar as your house address: "And we know that all things work together for good to those who love God, to those who are the called according to His purpose" (Romans 8:28).

John MacArthur describes Romans 8:28 as "breathtaking in its magnitude, encompassing absolutely everything that pertains to a believer's life."[1]

John Phillips observes that "like the cogs in an intricate piece of machinery, all things work together for good to the called of God for the simple reason that God's purposes cannot be thwarted."[2]

Maybe these patterns are like the cogs of a machine. But they're much more like a tremendous rock beneath your feet. When all the earth seems to tremble, and when nothing seems secure anymore, you can stand boldly on this rock, for no fault lines can dislodge it. No tremor can unsettle it. No, for this rock is set like a fine jewel within the shorelines of eternity, so that it is the tool of neither time nor space but only of the loving hand of God.

Let's explore five incredible truths from this awesome verse.

Romans 8:28 Is a Certain Promise

And we know . . .

Five times in the book of Romans, Paul will stand upon the assurance of *we know*. The apostle is really saying, "everyone knows" or, at least, "Christians know." It's a matter of common knowledge, a fact upon which everyone agrees.

Paul is not speculating that perhaps God is in control. He is reminding us that we know this for a certainty. Donald Barnhouse points out that "we know" may be the most excellent part of the verse. Finding out after the fact that everything was in the firm hand of God—well, that would be a wonderful thing. But God gives us that assurance *right now*. "To lay hold of that fact is to calm the turbulence of life and to bring quiet and confidence into the whole of life. Nothing can touch me unless it passes through the will of God."[3]

It is as if we are all characters in a suspense novel, when suddenly the apostle Paul sneaks in to whisper a word from the author. "The Novelist came up with an amazingly intricate plot," he says. "Everything comes out all right, though it gets a bit hairy for you in some of the chapters. When it all washes out, you're going to live happily ever after, and the villain will be punished."

It's a nice feeling to operate with inside information. Now all we have to do is get on with our scenes in the novel and a sly smile on our faces—a smile that says *we know.*

We know! But what *don't* we know?

"We do not know what we should pray for as we ought, but the Spirit Himself makes intercession for us with groanings which cannot be uttered" (Romans 8:26).

Can you see the pattern of verses 26–28? Paul is telling us there are things we can know, and things we cannot.

We can feel very good about the big picture (v. 28), but the little details are a mystery, for we don't know exactly what to pray for (v. 26). One of the greatest ironies of the Christian life is that we often have certainty about the ultimate and uncertainty about the immediate.

The truth is this: God is saying, "I want you to know right now that all of history, including the portion constituting your life, is completely under My control. No matter how things may appear, every little detail is part of a very beautiful picture. But I'm leaving those details as challenges of faith to prepare you for the world we will share one day. You must trust Me in those smaller things, knowing that the larger things are all established."

As we explore the many implications of this verse, let's say a word here about what it *does not* say:

- It does not say that everything will work out the way you'd like, if you'll only wait.
- It does not say that you can make things work out through positive thinking.
- It does not say that there's no point in what we do, because God pulls all the strings.

It *does* say that God is in control, but that He will intervene in this world to use every event as part of His comprehensive plan—His plan, but your ultimate good. He is working all the time, in all events, for the good of all believers: "For I am God, and there is no other; I am God, and there is none like Me, declaring the end from the beginning, and from ancient times things that are not yet done, saying, 'My counsel shall stand, and I will do all My pleasure.' . . . Indeed, I have spoken it; I will also bring it to pass. I have purposed it; I will also do it" (Isaiah 46:9–11).

Romans 8:28 Is a Comprehensive Promise

That all things . . .

Your Bible might translate these words as "all things" or "everything." Just as we discovered that "you know" is a blockbuster of a fact carried in only two words, the same thing happens here.

All things is our assurance that there are no limits. The offer is comprehensive and unconditional. No fine print. All sales are final. Or as we might say to the skeptic, "What part of 'all things' do you not understand?"

Please don't suspect Paul of being a cockeyed optimist, only considering the things in life that are already favorable. In this letter, as well as others, he discusses his many trials. In 2 Corinthians, as we saw in the last chapter, he offered an entire résumé of hard knocks. These were presented as his credentials for ministry. As recently as Romans 8:17, Paul has spoken of his "sufferings." We also hear of "groanings" in verse 23. But these miseries, too, are all part of that great plan that God is carrying out. Negative events have positive purposes.

But is Paul saying, "It's all good"? Is he claiming there's no such thing as evil, because of the final results?

Not at all. The death of a loved one is never a good thing, and the Spirit of God weeps beside us at the funeral. The terrible day you had yesterday is simply a terrible day. It felt bad; it *was* bad. The Romans 8:28 difference is that these are bad things that God *uses*. They are pieces of a great jigsaw puzzle that are ugly when considered on their own; but in the final picture, they will play a part that brings glory to God and works for the good of the believer.

Bad things, then, remain bad. But God remains good, and He is the Lord of those bad things. He is fully capable of using them in ways that will shine with a beauty we will see one day, either in this life or the next.

Paul uses the phrase *all things* several times in his letters. In each case, we come to understand that we serve a God of all things. There is nothing before us, nothing within us or outside us, nothing we can even imagine that is not His thing and usable within His plan.

We do well to look out upon this world from time to time and remind ourselves that we serve a sovereign God. He is the Lord of *all*. Everything in creation is no more, no less than the work of His hand. We have His promise "that in the dispensation of the fullness of the times He might gather together in one *all things* in Christ, both which are in heaven and which are on earth—in Him" (Ephesians 1:10, emphasis added).

Romans 8:28 Is a Complex Promise

. . . work together . . .

Paul looks out upon this shifting, changing, complex world and tells us that all things are working together.

This expression uses the Greek word *sunergeo*, from which we get our English word *synergism*: the working together of various elements to produce an effect greater than, and often completely different from, the sum of each element acting separately.

In the physical world, the right combination of otherwise harmful chemicals can produce substances that are of wonderfully positive use to us. For example, ordinary table salt is composed of two poisons: sodium and chlorine. Synergistically speaking, the final product is *much* better than the sum of its parts.

In the divine synergism, God mixes bitter herbs and spices with other tastier ingredients to create the perfect soup. Or, as Annie Johnson Flint has expressed it so beautifully in verse:

In a factory building there are wheels and gearings,
There are cranks and pulleys, beltings tight or slack—
Some are whirling swiftly, some are turning slowly,
Some are thrusting forward, some are pulling back;
Some are smooth and silent, some are rough and noisy,
Pounding, rattling, clanking, moving with a jerk;
In a wild confusion, in a seeming chaos,
Lifting, pushing, driving—but they do their work.
From the mightiest lever to the tiniest pinion,
All things move together for the purpose planned;
And behind the working is a mind controlling,
And a force directing, and a guiding hand.
So all things are working for the Lord's beloved;
Some things might be hurtful if alone they stood;
Some might seem to hinder; some might draw us backward;
But they work together, and they work for good,
All the thwarted longings, all the stern denials,
All the contradictions, hard to understand.

And the force that holds them, speeds them and retards them,
Stops and starts and guides them—is our Father's hand.[4]

Is our universe simply a finely tuned machine, and are we no better than its minor nuts and bolts? No, that is a gross, if common, misunderstanding of the beautiful doctrine of God's providence. We already know the beauty of the "machine" God has created: the rising and setting of the sun, the four seasons, the times of life. We observe the way we interact with one another as people—in marriage, in parenting, in friendship. All of these are the subtle workings of God's instrumentation. But the most beautiful part of all is that, unlike the machines we ourselves construct, this one has parts that act as free agents. The greatness of God is that He gives us freedom even within the delicate movements of a universe preset to accomplish His final purposes.

Romans 8:28 Is a Comforting Promise

. . . for good . . .

It's a wonderful thing to turn through the pages of our Bible and simply enjoy the promises that fill its pages. Throughout the Scriptures, God is telling us of all the good things He desires to give us, simply because He loves us so devotedly. The promises of God are good, because *He* is good—infinitely good. "Every good gift and every perfect gift is from above, and comes down from the Father of lights, with whom there is no variation or shadow of turning" (James 1:17).

When it comes to "good things," you and I see before us an embarrassment of riches. Try this experiment. Tomorrow morning, when you rise, take a pen and a small notepad in hand. As you move along, jot down every good thing in your life, whether it is some event or some thought or just something you see. If you need to get to work, I predict you'll never even get out of the house—you'll be too busy writing. God has loaded down your life and mine with the goodness of family, security, necessities, friends, interests, a beautiful world, and—well, if we start the list here, we'll never make it out of this chapter. See what I mean?

If you were to try that experiment, I think you would be forced to abandon it rather quickly. The thoughts would begin to come more and more quickly as you turned your heart in gratitude toward the Giver of these gifts. There is only one Giver, of course. It all comes from Him.

The problem is that we are so burdened with good gifts that when anything at all comes our way that isn't pleasant—so much as a traffic delay or a trip to the dentist—we throw our arms toward the sky and ask, "Why me?"

I'm not certain I've ever seen someone receive wonderful news— a job promotion or an accepted marriage proposal—and say, "Why me?" We take all these good gifts right in stride, as if we fully deserve them. Ask yourself these painful questions: Given the way we live our lives and the extent of our obedience to God, how many of these good things are we really earning? How many of the bad things are really unfair?

The point is not to feel guilty about our unworthiness. This is a book about grace! God has found a way to bless us despite our unworthiness. No, the point is that as much as God has showered us with good things, shouldn't we trust Him with the ones that seem questionable? If your dearest human friend always does nice things for you, you trust that person. How much greater trust does God deserve when He promises us that all things will eventually find their place in the machinery that brings forth what is best for us as we draw nearer and nearer to heaven?

There is also great encouragement in realizing that nothing is wasted. That's the testimony of this verse. God creates no waste, and He allows no waste. My friend Rob Suggs struggled through two disappointing careers before he found his calling as a writer at midlife. He knew that finally he was doing exactly what God had wanted him to do, but he felt deep regret that he hadn't found that path sooner. One day he was explaining his feelings to a friend. "All those years there was a Christian publishing company two miles from my house," he said. "I could have been working there for years, honing my skills, learning to do more for God. If only I had those years back—my twenties and my thirties."

His wise friend replied, "Don't you think that if God were in a hurry, He could have directed you two miles down the road several years earlier? The Lord had His timetable. He was using all your experiences, good and bad. Without them, you wouldn't be precisely the writer that you have become along your path."

And it's true. I have known many people who looked back upon their lives with regret. It brightens our hearts to know that God uses every last iota of every experience to move us toward the goal He has in mind.

And that goal is a good one. We can trust Him on that.

Romans 8:28 Is a Conditional Promise

> *. . . to those who love God to those who are the called according to His purpose.*

So what have we learned from Romans 8:28?

We know. We have inside knowledge.

All things. Everything, no exceptions.

Work together. It's all part of one perfect plan.

For good. We absolutely cannot lose.

This is one of the most *absolute* verses in all of Scripture. We absolutely know that absolutely all things work absolutely together for absolute good. It's absolutely wonderful! But now comes the part that is *not* absolute.

This promise does not apply to absolutely everyone. This is a highly significant consideration: the Romans 8:28 difference works exclusively for those who love God and are called for His purposes.

There are promises in Scripture that are unconditional, and some that have conditions. John 3:16, for example, holds one of each. "God so loved the world." That is an unconditional promise. He loves every single one of the children He created. We need to do nothing at all for Him to love us. "Whoever believes in Him should not perish but have everlasting life." That part is conditional. We will receive eternal life *if* we believe in Him.

His love, then, is unconditional. His gift of salvation has the one condition that we must believe.

In the same way, the promise of Romans 8:28 turns upon a condition. If we love God, then this wonderful, absolute principle takes effect for our lives. If we reject God, the events of life add up to a different conclusion altogether.

But you may have noticed there is an additional qualifier that describes those for whom this promise applies. It is for:

• Those who love God.

• Those who are the called according to His purpose.

Why does Paul set out that distinction? Aren't they the same people? Yes. Paul is describing the recipients of this blessing from two perspectives. The human angle is "those who love God." The divine angle is "those who are the called according to His purpose."

"Those who love God" are the ones who have chosen to identify with Him in this world. Paul shares another beautiful promise about those people: "Eye has not seen, nor ear heard, nor have entered into the heart of man the things which God has prepared for those who love Him" (1 Corinthians 2:9). We cannot imagine the wonderful gifts God has prepared for us. James 1:12 also tells us that God has prepared a "crown of life" to those who love Him.

"Those who are the called" are the same people, seen from God's perspective. There is a reminder here for us that, as wonderful as God's gifts are, we don't simply sit back in a recliner to selfishly enjoy them. In the instant of salvation, we receive our marching orders. We are on the move as we do our enjoying. We are called and appointed according to His purpose. He has work for us to do, and we are to be doing it all the days of our lives.

So Romans 8:28, like John 3:16, ends with a sobering reminder. There is one small item that qualifies us for the treasure that is described. We must believe in Him. We must love Him and receive His call.

The Romans 8:28 promise doesn't apply universally. But we should look at it this way: God himself excludes no one from receiving the benefits of any of His promises. It is people who tragically exclude themselves by failing to do the most natural thing in the world: to believe in and love the Lord, who is the source of every good thing. I can't imagine that any reasonable, clear-sighted person could help but love the God that you and I know, for to know Him is to love Him.

Therefore it's up to you and me to help those people know Him the way we do.

We know that God is good. We know He is working in this world. We know He is using all things for His purposes and for our good. And we know that someday we will stand beside His throne and see all of this world's events, and all the moments of our lives, from outside of time. We will see our birth, our death, and everything that came in between them as if it existed in one comprehensive mural. In that moment, all of the pieces of the puzzle will be seen in their true places and true functions. We'll know exactly what God had in mind and why He allowed the worst moments of our lives.

At that time, having been released once and for all from the blindness of self-absorption, we'll be able to look beyond ourselves. I think you and I will marvel at the interconnectedness of one human life to another, so that for the first time we'll be able to perceive how God affected us through other people, and how He used us in the lives of others.

We'll see that many things in this world were truly evil. We will have experienced a great deal of it ourselves. We will understand that He was never once the author of evil. But when we stand beside Him and look back at this world, seeing just how delicately and how wisely He put those evil elements to His own purpose—we will have no recourse but to fall on our knees and sing praises to Him.

We know this. We expect this. But what about now? Can we allow ourselves to be such total captives of His grace that we trust Him completely with life's most terrible moments?

Helen Roseveare was a British medical missionary in the Congo. She stayed at her post during some of the worst turmoil in the country's history in 1964. Many Westerners fled, but Helen believed she should be willing to make any sacrifice for a Savior who had made the ultimate sacrifice for her.

Someone tried to poison her, but her dog ate the food and the attempt failed. Still she stayed on. Female missionaries and medical personnel were often raped by rebel armies, but still she stayed on. Even when her house was looted of every item within it, she refused to leave her post.

It's not as if Helen had no fear. She rarely slept well, knowing that at any moment someone could enter her home and take her life. But she concentrated on learning to trust God more absolutely.

On Saturday, August 15, 1964, a truckload of soldiers commandeered her hospital. Helen would later recall, "They were brutal and coarse, rough and domineering. Their language was threatening and obscene. All of us were cowed. We did exactly what they demanded, mostly without argument." They caught the local chief, flayed him alive, and ate him.[5]

Eventually, Helen Roseveare was beaten, raped, and humiliated. Barely alive, she finally had to be taken from the country. During her long and painful days of recovery, she found herself closer to God than she had ever been before. She even loved the Congo more deeply than ever. There was no bitterness within her, though Helen had experienced terrible, mindless evil. It would have been so easy to demand of God why He allowed these atrocities, when she had been so faithful to His service. But in her heart of hearts, she felt that God's question would be, "Can you thank Me for trusting you with this experience, even if I never tell you why?"[6]

That question penetrates to the depth of our commitment to Christ. Yes, *we know* God is working all things for our good. Sometimes in this life we have the rare privilege of seeing just how God used this setback or that disappointment. We can feel the wisdom and strength that came through the basic trials of normal living. But can we trust Him even when we don't know the answers?

Paul sat in a prison cell and prayed fervently, hour after hour. There was so much work to be done. He had planted his share of churches, but most cities had still never heard the Gospel. He longed to go to Spain; surely it was God who placed that burden within his soul. And he needed to be with his brothers and sisters in the churches that were struggling. He loved them so deeply, and he longed to minister to them.

Yet God, who had shown He could easily crumble prison walls, would not effect Paul's release. Time was running out. Eventually he knew he would be executed. Surely God would rather have him on the front lines of the mission field, sharing the Gospel, rather than awaiting execution. Paul longed for freedom, but he simply trusted God.

John and Mary Newton longed for a family. For years they waited, trying to be patient, trying to conceive a child. Finally, after they had been married twenty-four years, the Lord sent them Elizabeth and Eliza in a very touching way. Mary Newton had lost a sister and a brother to tuberculosis, a deadly disease in that era. Each left behind one young daughter, and these became John and Mary Newton's adopted children.

Eliza, who was twelve when she joined the family, was often ill. The summer before her fifteenth birthday, Mary took her to Southampton, where the ocean air was thought to be healthier. Her husband wrote an encouraging letter, comparing the Southampton waters to the Pool of Bethesda in the Gospels. Maybe the Lord would work a healing miracle in Eliza's life.

But six weeks brought no improvement. Three weeks after returning to London with her mother, Eliza was dead.

Her grieving adoptive father prepared a little memorial book for the girl he had awaited for so long. In it he wrote: "If we know and trust Him . . . He chooses better for us than we can for ourselves . . . but now I can praise and adore Him for . . . His plan. I not only can bow . . . to His sovereignty, but I admire His wisdom and goodness, and can say from my heart, He has done all things well."[7]

Can you say that about your walk with God? Can you praise and adore Him even when your heart is breaking and you feel overwhelmed by disappointment? It could be that you're struggling with some trial at this very moment. If you can place your trust totally in His love and His promise to work all things for your good, then you will have taken a step toward embracing the mysteries of His grace.

You will bear a slightly closer resemblance to the Savior who gave His life to save you.

Then God will look upon your life, smile, and say, "Yes, My child. How you've grown since you first came to know Me! You're becoming wiser and stronger every day. There was a time when you could rejoice only when the sun was shining. But now your soul is taking on real substance. Now you are becoming sturdy and strong. I have trusted you with this burden, and you have honored Me through the stubbornness of your faith.

"Though your eyes are presently filled with tears, My child, and though your shoulders sag with unhappiness, I want you to know something. I want you to be assured that our adventure together is only beginning. Trials remain for you to face, but behind each one rests a greater glory. Beyond each obstacle there lies a greater joy. And all along the way, I have paved your road with blessings to remind you of the inheritance that is yours as My child. Walk on, now, in the joy that will not be slowed even by sadness. Walk on toward the crown of glory that has your name on it.

"Walk on, My child. And let us walk together."

Moments of Grace

Romans 8:28 is breathtaking in its magnitude and encompasses absolutely everything that could possibly happen to us. Every life event is turned inside out as part of God's comprehensive plan for the ultimate good of those who love Him. Even our sins, mistakes, and missteps. As a result of the total sweep of this promise, our hearts should be light as feathers and our joy should be boundless, grounded by faith in that all-pervasive promise.

If you've had a drooping attitude, try smiling right now—a big, face-wide grin. Tell your heart to cheer up. Command your emotions to soar to new, joyful levels. Take control of your feelings, and rejoice in Christ. Take it as a given that your current set of burdens will work out for good. Remember that discouragement is always from the devil, and make a choice to rejoice in the Lord "always"—and "always" means today!

PART THREE

GRACE
for the
FUTURE

CHAPTER NINE

The Compelling Prospect of Grace

When We've Been There Ten Thousand Years, Bright Shining As the Sun

John Newton had no problem with the idea of death. But retirement? He was opposed to the very thought of such a thing.

After all, who were these younger men who were coming around now, patting him on the shoulder as if he were an ancient relic? Bringing their not-so-subtle hints about slowing down, preaching more infrequently, allowing others to help him with his pastoral calls—why, he was at the height of his fruitfulness in the Gospel ministry. The Lord had lavished upon his heart a zeal that was still overflowing. Retire? He declined to entertain any consideration of the matter.

Even a dear old friend like Richard Cecil was working on him. It was Cecil's opinion that Newton should give up the pulpit entirely. "John, old boy," he said with a quiet voice and the usual pat on the shoulder. "Your sight is failing. Your hearing is nearly gone. I know you think you can be brave and cover it all up, but we are your friends. We have your best interests at heart. All things have their times and seasons under the sun, my friend—even old sea dogs in holy vestments. What will it take to slow you down? The Lord God sending Elijah to gather you up in His golden chariot?"

To which Newton could only snort with disdain and a raised voice, "What! Shall the old African blasphemer stop while he can speak?" And who would dare to answer that one?

Retirement—bah!

On the other hand, *death*: now, there was a subject worth talking about. Newton's letters and diary entries looked more and more to the hope of paradise that lay just over the horizon of his lifelong voyage. "The day of opportunity wears away, and the night is approaching," he wrote in 1802. Two years later, after signing a letter, he added: "Time, how short! Eternity, how long."[1]

His friends noticed in him a growing tendency toward morbid humor. He told one colleague that he was "packed, sealed, and waiting for the post."

While John Newton still possessed life and breath, however, he tended to his beloved sermons and hymns—"Amazing Grace" among the latter. Its final verse, as we've seen, would be filled in much later by another hand. But Newton did supply three verses we seldom use, and these provide a fine commentary on our present closing verse. They also demonstrate the extent to which Newton was eager for the comforts of the next world, even as a ship's captain watches anxiously for the farther shore through his spyglass:

> *The Lord has promised good to me,*
> *His word my hope secures;*
> *He will my shield and portion be,*
> *As long as life endures.*

Yes, when this flesh and heart shall fail,
And mortal life shall cease,
I shall possess, within the veil,
A life of joy and peace.

The earth shall soon dissolve like snow,
The sun forbear to shine;
But God, who call'd me here below,
Will be forever mine.

John Newton understood that life was, after all, a voyage from a familiar port to one unknown. He would no more dread the next world than he would resist steering his ship into the harbor toward which it was chartered.

When Newton finally passed on, he was given a Christian burial and a fitting epitaph upon the stone that marked his grave. But his loved ones might well have used the words of Paul to describe the life of John Newton: "For the grace of God that brings salvation has appeared to all men, teaching us that, denying ungodliness and worldly lusts, we should live soberly, righteously, and godly in the present age, looking for the blessed hope and glorious appearing of our great God and Savior Jesus Christ, who gave Himself for us, that He might redeem us from every lawless deed and purify for Himself His own special people, zealous for good works" (Titus 2:11–14).

It's uncertain whether Newton ever preached from this passage, but he surely cherished this thorough description of the work of God's grace. These verses demonstrate how that grace is with us in the past, the present, and the future:

• It has appeared to all men.
• It appears now for teaching.
• It will appear again in the return of Christ.

John Newton and Paul the apostle were both captured by the timelessness of that grace. Neither ever lost sight of how Christ had intercepted their self-destructive courses in the past. Both men found His redemptive grace in every aspect of their present, and both men actively awaited a future in which the grace of the Lord would find its final and ultimate culmination.

Paul might have spoken for both men when he wrote, "By the grace of God I am what I am, and His grace toward me was not in vain" (1 Corinthians 15:10). Grace was no isolated theme; it was the whole story. These men understood themselves completely through the lens of God's redemptive grace.

GRACE TEACHES US

Paul explains to Titus that the grace of God has *appeared*. The Greek word translated "appeared" gives us our modern word *epiphany*—a wonderful word. We use it in a secular way to describe a sudden and intense realization of truth. An epiphany is that proverbial light bulb appearing over your head, but lit by solar power!

When the Greeks spoke of an epiphany, they were referring to the breathtaking view of sunlight bursting in power over the edge of the world to illuminate the darkened earth. The grace of God, Paul tells us, has suddenly brought light to our world after thousands of years of darkness. It explodes upon the world with awesome power, providing humanity with an intense realization of the nature of God.

In several other passages (particularly in the three pastoral epistles, 1 and 2 Timothy and Titus), Paul returns to this idea of the bright epiphany of our Savior. A lovely comparison: before the rising sun or the risen Son, we are humbled and grateful. Both are miracles completely outside our control; our physical and spiritual survival, respectively, depend upon them. God's grace is His gift to a helpless and dying planet.

That "epiphany," for Paul, is the birth of Christ in Bethlehem. There is ultimate grace in God appearing in flesh among the poor. There is breathtaking grace in God becoming a helpless child, entering the world in a cattle shed with shepherds to greet His coming. From there, every aspect of the life of Jesus communicates grace: Jesus healing the sick; Jesus befriending sinners; Jesus teaching love and forgiveness, rather than playing on the public's anger and rebellion against Roman authority. Finally Jesus submits to a shameful death and forgives His very executioners from the cross. But the best is yet to come. In the Resurrection, we find the culmination of the gift of grace—victory over death is God's ultimate gift of grace to His undeserving children.

In Christ, the grace of God is made manifest. If love is the attribute that describes God the best, grace is the one that makes that love obtainable for us. Grace is the most radical concept ever to be introduced into this world. It is counterintuitive to human nature, challenging every human tendency and providing the solution for every human problem.

Grace changes people as nothing else can do. It cleanses the sins of the past. It enables righteousness in the present. And one thing it does for certain: it constantly surprises us. For the essence of grace is surprise. There is nothing shocking about giving people exactly what they deserve. Grace subverts the rules and gives people what they *don't* deserve. It is motivated by the warmth of love rather than by cold calculation. Therefore, grace is always doing something we didn't expect.

For example, what does grace do in the present? It walks to the blackboard and begins to teach: "For the grace of God that brings salvation has appeared to all men, teaching us" (Titus 2:11–12).

Paul tells us that the grace of God appears to all men and then instantly begins the lesson. After all, we find ourselves living here in the present. We look backward at the first appearance of grace, when Christ was born in Bethlehem in the darkness of a sinful world; we look forward to the glorious appearing of Christ at the end of time, when we will be made perfect. But what about now? We need to know how to live in the interim. Grace, through the power and guidance of the Holy Spirit, is here to help us live. It therefore clears its throat and begins our education.

Let's discover what lessons are included in the curriculum of Grace University.

Grace Teaches Us to Renounce Sin

> *Denying ungodliness and worldly lusts . . .*
> —TITUS 2:12

The first lesson of grace is about denial. Grace wants to usher us toward a new life, one of purity and righteousness. The first consideration is dealing with the problems of the old life that cannot accompany us on that journey. Our word for *denial* comes from the Greek word for *disown*. It is as if you are grabbing an old habit by its ear, taking it to the front door, and depositing it outdoors to be picked up with the trash. To disown is to detach completely. It is to say, "I will not own any problem that begins to own me."

But let's allow Paul to explain it for us. This concept of denying ungodliness carries over to the next chapter of Paul's letter to Titus:

For we ourselves were also once foolish, disobedient, deceived, serving various lusts and pleasures, living in malice and envy, hateful and hating one another. But when the kindness and love of God our Savior toward man appeared, not by works of righteousness

which we have done, but according to His mercy He saved us, through the washing of regeneration and renewing of the Holy Spirit, whom He poured out on us abundantly through Jesus Christ our Savior, that having been justified by His grace we should become heirs according to the hope of eternal life. This is a faithful saying, and these things I want you to affirm constantly, that those who have believed in God should be careful to maintain good works. These things are good and profitable to men. (Titus 3:3–8)

In summary, it's as if to say the wealthiest man in the province has come to the city and seen the worst social reprobates imaginable, luxuriating in dark alleys like pigs in a trough. These are vagrants guilty of every offense. He has gone down into the grime, getting their filth all over himself, in order to pull them out of the alley and escort them home to his palatial manor. There he has washed them by his own hand, fed them, clothed them, and whispered words of hope and a future to them. Then he has told them they were adopted as his children. Everything he has is theirs.

Those adopted sons and daughters would surely be moved to the depths of their souls. You wouldn't expect to find them sneaking back to their sordid dens of corruption, would you? Not when the glorious riches and friendship of the master are available.

Needless to say, it is you and I who have been cleaned, fed, clothed, and adopted. Why in creation would we wish to live by the decadent trappings of the old life? Grace, having cleansed us, should now live within us, giving us new desires and values.

When I watched Mel Gibson's movie *The Passion of the Christ*, I was astounded by the emotions that rose up within me. The most powerful and least expected of all, however—and the one that had the most lasting influence upon me—was this thought: *Because of what Christ did for me, I don't want to ever do anything to bring shame or hurt to Him.* Watching with my own eyes an approximation of His suffering on my behalf provided a new and more powerful motivation to live a holy life.

Many of us forget what has been done for us. We forget the pain He accepted on our behalf, and we forget that we are delivered to the possibility of a new life, one so much more joyful and rewarding.

Grace Teaches Us to Rule Self

We should live soberly . . .
—Titus 2:12

In our new life in the Master's house, we will want to deny "ungodliness and worldly lust." How then shall we live? *Soberly.*

This is a very crucial New Testament concept that many of us need to study more closely. A good translation of that word would be "with self-control." Spiritual sobriety is the maturity to exercise sound mind and judgment. It is inner self-government that reins in all the passions and desires that war against us. The grace-driven believer disciplines his passions as a military leader would discipline his troops. And what passions? Eating, sleeping, talking, playing. The Spirit of God will point you to the specific issues of your own life. The idea is that the poor, rescued reprobate will not only give up the old, worthless pursuits; he will exercise wisdom and restraint in the new choices he makes of his time.

Throughout his letters to Timothy and Titus, Paul mentions this sobriety as a character trait required of pastors as well as men and women, young and old. In other words, every Christian should be showing constant growth in the area of sober living. Remember that self-control is a fruit of the Spirit. Are you seeing the fruit in your own life?

The Jews of New Testament times had a wonderful word picture that accompanied the concept of sobriety. It was to "gird up the loins of your mind." Remember how the father of the Prodigal had to run to meet his son? Gym shorts were not available, so the runner had to gather up his robe about him to allow his legs to move forward with power. Sobriety is gathering our wits, getting the impediments out of the way, and moving forward much more rapidly. Your life and mine should follow the model.

Let's also take a look at three situations calling for sober-mindedness:

1. *In anticipation of Christ's revelation.* "Therefore gird up the loins of your mind, be sober, and rest your hope fully upon the grace that is to be brought to you at the revelation of Jesus Christ" (1 Peter 1:13).

2. *In preparation for Satan's temptation.* "Be sober, be vigilant; because your adversary the devil walks about like a roaring lion, seeking whom he may devour" (1 Peter 5:8).

3. *In evaluation of our place in fellowship.* "For I say, through the grace given to me, to everyone who is among you, not to think of himself more highly than he ought to think, but to think soberly, as God has dealt to each one a measure of faith" (Romans 12:3).

We are called, therefore, to be serious and disciplined in mind and spirit, to wait on the Lord, to fight off temptation, and to serve the church. Imagine what your life could be if you became strategic about girding up the loins of your mind. How fast would you run?

Grace Teaches Us to Respect Others

We should live . . . righteously . . .
—Titus 2:12

Grace, by its very essence, is unselfish. It follows Paul's guidance in Philippians 2:3 to "let nothing be done through selfish ambition or conceit, but in lowliness of mind let each esteem others better than himself."

Can you imagine a world where respectful behavior is normal? The loss of simple, civil respect is one of the symptoms of how far we have fallen as a society. We see the loss of respect for figures of authority, for elders, and for sacred matters of faith (whether our own belief or the beliefs of others). Our children watch television programs that encourage them to speak their mind, to have an attitude, and to do whatever they want to do. We notice that nothing is ever said about basic respect.

The grace life respects not only elders and people of authority but everyone it encounters. It respects those with whom we disagree. It respects strangers. In work situations, it respects subordinates. When we live by grace, we see through the eyes of grace. Suddenly that other person appears to us as a child of God, someone to whom Christ is reaching out, just as He is reaching to us. We hear His voice whispering to us, "Will you help Me get through to that one? Will you serve this person? She cannot hear my voice now, but she will respond to your gentleness."

Respect is the key that opens the door to any relationship. If you want to connect with someone hard to reach, take time to express words that demonstrate respect. If you want to end an argument very quickly, show respect.

Try the power of the respect principle with an elementary-level child sometime. Children feel very small. When you stop to speak to them and address them not in condescending grownup talk, but as you would talk to anyone else, you will make a friend forever. Jesus insisted on giving children love and time even when His disciples tried to push them away. The grace of Christ respects everyone. He focused on what they had that was special (in their case, childlike faith). Grace does that well. It finds what is worthy and respectable in every human being and honors it.

You can learn to relate to people this way. Let grace be your teacher.

Grace Teaches Us to Reverence God

> *We should live [in a manner that is] godly in the present age . . .*
> —TITUS 2:12

Paul is always very logical in the procession of his ideas. He has told us to live soberly (the inward life). He has told us to live righteously (the outward life). Now he tells us to live in a way that is godly (the upward life).

The Greek word translated "godliness" is *eusebeia.* It is used frequently in the letters to Timothy and Titus. "Godliness" in these verses means piety and reverence toward God. We devote ourselves to Him and to His will in our hearts, our heads, and with our hands.

We've all known godly men and women, and immediately we admire them. How did they get to be that way? Were they godly at birth?

The answer is that the grace of God teaches godliness. Every day, as we listen to His voice, as He convicts us of sin and encourages us toward service, as He brings out the fruit promised in Galatians 5:22–23, as He molds us to the image of Christ—all this time we are growing in godliness. Of course, not everyone has the same growth rate. There are those who stop right at the gate of salvation and never go more than a step or two deeper into Christian maturity. This is like being adopted into the Master's family and insisting on sleeping in the garage and eating from the garbage can. A feast has been set for us, and the Spirit feeds it to us bite by bite.

I used to think that godliness was an impossible goal, if not for everyone, at least for me. And then I read these words in 2 Peter: "His divine power has given to us all things that pertain to life and godliness, through the knowledge of Him who called us by glory and virtue, by which have been given to us exceedingly great and precious promises, that through these you may be partakers of the divine nature, having escaped the corruption that is in the world through lust" (1:3–4).

Not only is godliness within reach, but everything we need to achieve it has already been given to us in the "exceedingly great and precious promises" of God's Word.

So what is holding us back? What keeps us from the goal of godliness? The disconnect is not God's but ours. Paul tells us that becoming godly is hard work, that it requires our disciplined effort. "Exercise yourself toward godliness. For bodily exercise profits a little, but godliness is profitable for all things, having promise of the life that now is and of that which is to come" (1 Timothy 4:7–8).

I believe this is what Paul is talking about when he tells the Philippians to work out their own salvation with fear and trembling (Philippians 2:12).

Grace Teaches Us to Respond Diligently

Zealous for good works . . .
—Titus 2:14

God's grace always results in good works. Once again, imagine coming to live in that wonderful mansion. The Master is with you always, but He is constantly asking you to run "errands" with Him. What are these errands? He's constantly paying little visits of service to other people. He saves other lives like your own. He continues to give gifts and loving friendship to you. He does everything He can to make the world a better place.

Now imagine living within the scope of that influence and failing to have it rub off on you. No one but someone with the hardest of hearts could avoid falling right into step with the Master and helping Him to do all that can be done. Why, after a while, you might have the idea of getting organized about it. You'd call together all the former reprobates from the dark alleys and say, "Let's fan out and get as much done in this city as we can. Some of us will work nearby, feeding and clothing and helping; others will go out of town and get to work. Think of how much we can get done!"

Yet inevitably there would be someone who says, "Go ahead, knock yourself out, my friend. I'm not much on that service stuff. I'm going to hang around the mansion and watch television."

Now I ask you, could that person be in touch with his inner grace? Especially since the others would be discovering that service was the greatest gift of all from their Master. Service completes our joy. It uses the spiritual gifts that we were made to use, so that nothing else can provide so much fulfillment. That's called being "zealous for good works."

Isn't it interesting that Paul gives the strongest statement in the Bible concerning the nature of salvation by grace through faith: "For by grace you have been saved through faith, and that not of yourselves" (Ephesians 2:8). Then, in the very next breath, he adds: "For we are His workmanship, created in Christ Jesus for good works, which God prepared beforehand that we should walk in them" (Ephesians 2:10).

He has been making the powerful point that our own works cannot save us. Only His grace can do that. But what were we created for? Works! He does the saving, and we do the serving. That's how it was meant to be.

Paul bears testimony of this principle in his own life: "But by the grace of God I am what I am, and His grace toward me was not in vain; but I labored more abundantly than they all, yet not I, but the grace of God which was with me" (1 Corinthians 15:10).

Watching for the Blessed Hope

Looking for the blessed hope and glorious appearing of our
great God and Savior Jesus Christ.
—TITUS 2:13

Paul gives us the picture of someone keeping watch, like the father of the Prodigal Son. The grace life keeps hope alive in the human heart. We begin to see more and more through the eyes of heaven, just as John Newton did as he grew older. Retirement seems distasteful, for God's work is never done and we were created for good works. Death, on the other hand, means heaven. To live is Christ; to die is gain. In their old age, these two men, Paul the apostle and Newton the navigator, began to look more and more alike—just as all of us begin to show the family resemblance after years of being daily molded more and more to His image.

Meanwhile, through the eyes of heaven there is always hope. We realize that our actions now can bear fruit years, generations, even centuries after our lives. Newton's most famous fruit, of course, is "Amazing Grace." But I believe he would have been even more satisfied with an influence he had that is less widely known.

In the year 1759, as John Newton was beginning to adapt to life after sailing, a man was born by the name of William Wilberforce. He was born wealthy and had a winning personality. As he grew to manhood, he was attracted to the political life. But he could find no peace within himself. He gradually became more and more certain that God had a higher calling for him. When he was twenty-one years old and still processing what the future might hold for him, he was a member of Parliament. Wilberforce began to attend a church in London, St. Mary Woolnoth. The rector there was a man by the name of John Newton.

It was impossible to know Newton without knowing about the past that still plagued his memories. He would preach about his days as a slave trader, and about how God had come to show him the inhumanity of buying and selling human beings. At this time, in 1780, many agreed that slavery was a problem, but most people doubted that anything could be done about it.

Newton spoke the conscience of God on the subject. The young Wilberforce listened carefully. There was a new friendship between the old captain and the young idealist. Newton fanned Wilberforce's gifts into flame and convinced him that his political life could be used for the service of God's kingdom. More and more, the passion for the abolition of slavery took hold of William Wilberforce. As he grew older, he became England's leader in the movement to abolish British slavery. After a battle that lasted eighteen years, the slave trade itself was abolished.

Then, three days before Wilberforce's death in 1833, the House of Commons passed the law that emancipated all slaves in British colonies. Within twenty years, the influence had become so powerful in America that slavery was abolished there too.

Newton was right—there is nothing more amazing than grace. It isn't content to take hold of our lives and change us from the inside out. It then reaches through us to change everyone in the world that it can.

Even as John Newton anticipated the joys of heaven, God was using him to spread good works in this world. His legacy today is both song and freedom—two things that match quite well. His last recorded words were "I am satisfied with the Lord's will."[2]

His epitaph reads as follows:

> *JOHN NEWTON*
> *Clerk*
> *Once an infidel and libertine,*
> *a servant of slaves in Africa,*
> *was, by the rich mercy of our Lord and Savior,*
> *JESUS CHRIST,*
> *preserved, restored, pardoned,*
> *and appointed to preach the faith,*
> *he had long labored to destroy.*
> *He ministered near sixteen years as curate and vicar,*
> *Of Olney in Bucks*
> *and twenty-eight years as rector of these united parishes.*
> *On February 1, 1750, he married*
> *MARY,*
> *daughter of the late George Catlett,*
> *of Chatham, Kent,*
> *whom he resigned to the Lord who gave her,*
> *on December 15, 1790*

John Newton hasn't been there ten thousand years, by our reckoning. But then again, in the new home he has found, there is no measurement of years or of moments. We know that time and space are creations of God only for this world. When we go to the mansions Christ has prepared for us, one moment will be as a thousand years, and a thousand years as a moment (2 Peter 3:8).

I imagine that two men, the personal subjects of this book, are beloved friends in that world. What conversations they must have together!

Newton's epitaph above includes the words:

appointed to preach the faith,
he had long labored to destroy.

It's easy to imagine Paul asking him about those words. "You could have done no more toward being an enemy of the faith than I did," Paul might say.

And perhaps Newton, as overflowing with grace as ever, would reply, "All of us were equally enemies of the faith who were well-deserving of our death, but for the love and mercy of God. I pursued free men to imprison them in slavery. You pursued believers to imprison them in Jerusalem. Praise God that He pursued us more relentlessly, more devotedly, more lovingly. Praise God that we were captured by grace. And let us worship His name that He freed us from the slavery we had imposed upon ourselves."

And upon those words, I'm quite certain that the two men, the two brothers, the two eternal children in Christ would turn again to the throne where sits the King of kings, the Lord of creation. And they would add their voices to the song of the angels, exalting the One whose grace is deep enough and wide enough to rescue every single one of us.

Moments of Grace

Think of the self-control aspect of grace—the grace of God teaches us to deny ungodliness and worldly lusts and to live self-controlled in this present world. What one single habit in your life most needs to be captured by the grace of God? Is it overeating? Swearing? Lust? A short temper?

To practice self-control in this area, use the Six-C Method: Determine to bring every thought and habit under *captivity* to Christ. *Confess* it to God in a specific prayer of repentance. *Claim* the victory from God on the basis of His great and precious promises. *Confide* this matter to a friend who will serve as your accountability partner. And *continue*, no matter what—don't give in or give up, even if you have failures along the way. God's grace is stronger than your weakness, and His blood not only forgives you; it *cleanses* from all sin (1 John 1:9).

CHAPTER TEN

The Continual Praise *of* Grace

We've No Less Days to Sing God's Praise Than When We First Begun

E ternity.

It excites hope and defies understanding.

Maybe if we could envision—just a little—what that world will be like, we would no longer fear death. Perhaps if our limited minds could manage to hold the briefest glimpse of paradise, the conception would change everything about the way we live now.

But that would be like a teacup trying to hold the Pacific Ocean. We might as well try wrapping our arms around the Milky Way galaxy, and a grasshopper might as well try to understand quantum physics. No matter how much we try, we cannot begin to comprehend the nature of that final blessed destination, when all the obstacles of our fallen human nature will finally be removed. We see now in a mirror darkly, but then we will see face to Face.

What will it be like to experience "forever"? *When we've been there ten thousand years.* Even as those words thrill us, we recognize their limitations. Time is a creation of God, like stars or starfish. When we take our first eager step into that next and higher world, time will be no more. A moment will be as ten thousand years, and ten thousand years as a moment.

But of course the poet understands that, for the following line expresses the idea of eternity superbly: "We've no less days to sing God's praise than when we first begun." We will have the bounds of eternity to praise and worship the Name that is above all names. But even that solid biblical truth creates a challenge of comprehension for many of us. There are some who hesitantly ask, "Will we really be singing for all of eternity? Couldn't it get—um, tiresome?

The reason we stumble over that one is that we can no more understand perfect gratitude than we can understand the perfect love that inspires it. We were created to exalt the Lord. In the act of worship we find our ultimate fulfillment, as a horse finds its place in running or an eagle in flight. Perhaps the idea of eternal praise giving is such a foreign one because wholehearted worship in *this* world is equally strange to us.

But if you want that briefest glimpse of eternity; if you want the foretaste of glory divine—then worship is the one channel for approaching the throne of God. And it comes at that still point where grace meets gratitude.

After all, what is Newton's great hymn but a song of grace wrapped in gratitude? How do you respond when you receive an unexpected, unmerited, and beautiful gift? You feel humbled. You feel uplifted. You feel that more than anything else, you want to express your thanks in the most profound way you can find. Placing the matter in mathematical terms, if the response of gratitude is proportional to the value of grace, then we are thankful when someone brings us a cup of cold water, we are overjoyed to receive a gift of unexpected wealth, and we are infinitely and eternally grateful when someone rescues us from death and despair.

The idea of ingratitude, in the light of what we have received, is worse than unthinkable.

Consider that Paul lists ingratitude as a hallmark of the world's last days. Do you recognize the following description of a culture on the verge of collapse? "But know this, that in the last days perilous times will come: For men will be lovers of themselves, lovers of money, boasters, proud, blasphemers, disobedient to parents, unthankful, unholy" (2 Timothy 3:1–2).

I think we can all agree that complaining is a contagion of our times. My friend James MacDonald undertook a study of Internet sites that have been set up just for complainers. One of them is The Complaint Station, which claims to have served five million whiners. Another site seems to understand griping as one of life's greatest joys:

> Complain about anything. The whole world is here to listen. Complain about your neighbor. Complain about the airlines. Complain about trains. Complain about noise. Complain about your mother-in-law. Complain about high prices. About getting ripped off. About potholes. About police. Complain about welfare. Complain about work. Complain about your boss. Complain to us. We'll listen and tell everyone. No exceptions! [1]

There are even Christian complaint sites, believe it or not. You can complain that Bible college is too expensive or that nonbelievers curse too much. You can vent about those pastors and church staff members who really bother you. It's difficult to imagine how any follower of Jesus Christ would believe that complaining was a worthwhile or edifying pursuit.

Would you rather be around people who are hateful or grateful? Consider a recent scholarly study on the results of gratitude. It's a bit more difficult to find Web sites devoted to thankfulness than those given to complaining. Yet this 2003 research concluded that grateful people receive a wide range of benefits simply because of their perspective on life. They sleep better and enjoy better physical health. Their social relationships are enhanced. They have a deeper and rewarding sense of spirituality. "Gratitude not only makes people feel good in the present, but it also increases the likelihood that people will function optimally and feel good in the future."[2] Gratitude is one heaping helping of wellness—something more beneficial than ten thousand vitamins or ten years of workouts at the gym.

Grace should create gratitude. And gratitude simply makes the world a far more positive place. It's not surprising to find that the apostle of grace has a great deal to say about the spirit of gratitude.

Praise Priority

In everything give thanks; for this is the will of God in Christ Jesus for you.
—I Thessalonians 5:18

The word *joy* occurs 181 times in the Bible, and the word *thanksgiving*, which appears in one of its various forms some 136 times, is woven tightly throughout the fabric of Scripture.

In the Old Testament, the grace of gratitude was given such prominence that certain members of the priesthood were assigned the sole task of leading the congregation in expressing it. For example, when Nehemiah's workers finally completed rebuilding the wall around Jerusalem, they recognized the moment with a service of thanksgiving: "Now at the dedication of the wall of Jerusalem they sought out the Levites in all their places, to bring them to Jerusalem to celebrate the dedication with gladness, both with thanksgivings and singing, with cymbals and stringed instruments and harps" (Nehemiah 12:27).

On at least two occasions, the Bible links the spirit of grateful praise with the victorious Christian life: "Now thanks be to God who always leads us in triumph in Christ" (2 Corinthians 2:14). "But thanks be to God, who gives us the victory through our Lord Jesus Christ" (1 Corinthians 15:57).

William Law, writing centuries ago, said, "Would you know who is the greatest saint in the world? It is not he who prays most or fasts most, it is not he who gives alms most,…but it is he who is always thankful to God,…who receives everything as an instance of God's goodness and has a heart always ready to praise God for it."

Praise Perspective

In the Old Testament, the prophet Samuel exhorted the people of God with these words: "Only fear the LORD, and serve Him in truth with all your heart; for consider what great things He has done for you" (1 Samuel 12:24).

Shouldn't each one of us be instituting a personal service of thanksgiving on a daily basis? Consider these gifts of grace for which we rarely take time to be grateful:

- If you own just one Bible, you are abundantly blessed. Most people in the world do not.
- If you awoke this morning more healthy than ill, you are more blessed than one million people who will not survive the week.
- If you have never experienced the danger of battle, the loneliness of imprisonment, the agony of torture, or the pangs of starvation, you are ahead of more than five hundred million people around the world.

- If you have food in your refrigerator, clothes on your back, a roof over your head, and a place to sleep, you are richer than 75 percent of this world.
- If you have money in the bank, in your wallet, and spare change in a dish somewhere, you are among the top 8 percent of the world's wealthy.
- If you prayed yesterday and today, you are in the minority because you believe in God's willingness to hear and answer prayer.
- If you have the ability to choose between churches where you may freely worship, you have a blessing many people in this world do not.
- If you are a devoted follower of Jesus Christ, you live with the daily assurance that you will have eternal life, and that your Savior has gone to prepare a mansion for you in glory. Millions of people believe this sad life is all there is.[3]

Helen Keller made a compelling observation: "I have often thought it would be a blessing if each human being were stricken blind and deaf for a few days at some time early in adult life. Darkness would make him more appreciative of sight and silence would teach him the joys of sound."[4]

Imagine your life devoid of gratitude. It would be a life completely lacking any healthy perspective. It would be capable of seeing only problems. It would be dominated by fear, anxiety, stress, and ultimately the dark cloak of depression. In short, a life without gratitude would be a kind of living death.

Praise God that His grace has broken through to us. The death and resurrection of His Son have rescued us from that darkness, and His Holy Spirit has come to live within us, encouraging our hearts each day toward every positive emotion. The benefits of being a serious disciple create a spiral of gratitude that should break out of the shells of our lives and flood the surrounding landscape with eternal light.

The more we think of God, the more we thank Him. Those two verbs come from the same root, by the way. Right thinking leads to bright thanking ("bright shining as the sun").

PRAISE POSSIBILITIES

Giving thanks always for all things to God the Father in the name of our Lord Jesus Christ.
—EPHESIANS 5:20

Whatever you do in word or deed, do all in the name of the Lord Jesus,
giving thanks to God the Father through Him.
—COLOSSIANS 3:17

In Ephesians, Paul instructs us to give thanks to God for all things. In Colossians, he tells us what he means by "all things": every act and every word.

If you want the model for how to live that way, look no further than Paul himself. He had a gratitude that followed him to his last days of imprisonment, illness, and even criticism by other Christians of his time. It's impossible to write the word *thanksgiving* over and over when it isn't engraved in your mind-set. Paul wrote four of his letters from prison, and every one of them carries the word *thanksgiving*. He mentions gratitude ten times in all.

Now consider that model for personal comparison. If we could see a transcript of all the words you have spoken over the past month, what would that verbiage reveal about your character? And what would happen if you were suddenly thrown into prison unfairly? What is your honest feeling about where your words and letters would fall on the positive/negative continuum? The words that proceed from our mouths say a great deal about who we are and what mind-set we carry through life; the setting from which we say those words says even more.

People tell me, "I agree that I should count my blessings. But if you only knew what my life was like right now—I've had a really down year. I've been victimized by all kinds of people and circumstances."

Paul and many, many other men and women from the early church suffered far more deeply than we have in those times we perceive to be tough. Perspective makes a great deal of difference, doesn't it? In our country, there are countless people who enjoy three meals a day with shelter over their heads yet spend their lives believing they're not well off. They see the mansions on the other side of town and feel deprived for being in the top 97 percent of the world's affluent and not the top 99.

Paul was stoned at Lystra, driven out of Thessalonica, rejected by the Athenians, jailed by the Philippians, apprehended by the Caesareans, carried in chains to Rome, and shipwrecked on the way. He was released and imprisoned again, thrown in a dungeon, and martyred for his faith. He lived with a daily infirmity of some kind (his "thorn in the flesh") that brought regular misery. And not a bit of any of it dampened his gratitude to God. Should we be surprised? Only if we make the tremendous error of connecting gratitude and joy to mere circumstances. Faith, hope, love, and gratitude are faith attributes we hold regardless of circumstances.

The most powerful expression of that idea once again comes from Paul. He offered the Romans a list of negative experiences that Christians could and did encounter: tribulation, distress, persecution, famine, nakedness, peril, and sword. Then he concluded: "Yet in all these things we are more than conquerors through Him who loved us" (Romans 8:37).

Paul takes his stand at the very crosshairs of the devil's target and says, "I'm here. Let the world, the flesh, and the devil hurl every possible weapon at me. Remove every luxury I have, as happened to Job. Try me to the point of distress, as happened to Abraham. Let me stumble on the impediments of my own sinful appetites, as happened to David. I could even deny the Lord as Peter denied Him, and still the Lord would never deny me. For nothing, and I mean *nothing*, can separate me from the love of Christ. Nothing will deny me from being the conqueror that Christ has made me to be through the power and redemption of His love. For that reason, I can be strong. I can be courageous. I can stand against anything that stands against me, because I have the advantage of knowing I will win in the end through the victorious blood of my Savior; that no matter what happens to me here on earth, I will come before Him in the day of judgment and be declared *justified* because the Son has stood in my place. Therefore I will laugh and sing with the joy of heaven through the worst of storms, and just try to stop me! I will live every moment in the abundance of gratitude that flows from the power of grace."

Dr. Lee Salk was an eminent child and family authority who died in 1992. He loved to speak of his mother's experiences growing up in Russia. As a girl, she was driven from her home by Cossacks. As the attacking mob burned the village to the ground, she fled for her life, hiding in hay wagons and huddling in ditches. Eventually, crowded in a ship's hold, she crossed the sea to America.

Several years ago, a story in *Guideposts* magazine related the story behind Dr. Salk's famous quote: "Even after my mother married and her sons were born . . . it was still a struggle to keep food on the table. . . . But my mother urged us to think about what we had, not what we didn't have. She taught us that in hardship you develop a capacity to appreciate the beauty that exists in the simplest elements of life. The attitude that she so fiercely conveyed to us was this: When it gets dark enough, you can see the stars."

PRAISE PERFECTION

I will sing of the mercies of the LORD forever.
—PSALM 89:1

We can imagine two very similar figures, separated only by the centuries and the miles: John Newton dozing by his fire, Paul leaning against the cold wall of his cell. We can imagine both men allowing their thoughts to escape the confines of their aging bodies and drift to heaven, where the culmination of their lives and hopes would finally arrive. Since the day of rebirth for each—one tossed from a horse, one tossed by a storm at sea—these two had offered continuous praise and thanksgiving to the One who sent grace in pursuit of them. Both men could imagine what it would be like to finally say thank you face to Face, from within the veil of holiness rather than beyond this veil of tears. They could see themselves in the guise of the apostle John, standing there at the doorway to heaven in the beloved disciple's apocalyptic vision in Revelation 11:16–17:

> *And the twenty-four elders who sat before God on their thrones fell*
> *on their faces and worshiped God, saying:*
>
> *"We give You thanks, O Lord God Almighty,*
> *The One who is and who was and who is to come,*
> *Because You have taken Your great power and reigned."*

My friend, do you ever daydream about that eventuality? Do you ever allow your heart to roam beyond the shackles of this dark world, into the realm of pure light, bright shining as the sun, where our Savior dwells? It is no idle dream but our firm destiny. It is the end result to which every moment and every activity of this life should point like a neon signpost in the desert.

In the meantime, however, this earth will have to do. We are called to live in a fallen world, but His grace is sufficient—as it was for Paul, as it was for John Newton. Each found joy, peace, and new life in the love of Christ that covered the shame of their pasts. I wonder if you have experienced that level of victory over your own history of struggles. I wonder if the grace of Christ is proving sufficient to you in those current challenges that threaten to bring you anxiety and rob you of sleep.

What a tragedy if a single one of us lived within arm's reach of the grace of God and never took it in hand to experience its tremendous power. I have experienced the sufficiency of God's grace over and over in my own life, including those moments when I battled cancer through chemotherapy. What I discovered is that Paul is absolutely correct: nothing can separate us from the love of Christ. Nothing can even come close. The extent of our challenge defines the extent to which God is glorified, and you are blessed as you cling more tightly to Him through the storm.

Grace is a powerful force whose path can be traced through this world. It cuts a swath through the heaviest fortifications of the devil, when Christians merely wake up and begin to trust in the power of their Savior. I would offer the most fitting example to close a book that has followed the journeys of Paul and Newton by land, sea, and spirit.

The story begins at the foot of the cross, where grace covered all of humanity's sin and began to travel its path of redemption through our world.

The story continues as grace pursues Paul until he is radically changed inside. It inspires him to write the most hopeful letters ever written—powerful epistles of grace.

We follow the path of grace into the eighteenth century, where it overtakes a slave trader at the depth of despair. First he finds grace for his own sins, and eventually he understands that grace applies also to the African slaves who are being bought and sold.

Only a few years pass before we find a young man named William Wilberforce, who is captured by grace himself. John Newton, in the fullness of his years, can do little to make a difference in the English slave trade. But Wilberforce, a rising star in Parliament, will finally see the blot of slavery erased from British practice.

Finally we follow the path of grace across the sea. The story of the hymn will find its culmination in word and influence simultaneously. The path leads to the door of a young lady in Cincinnati, Ohio, at the middle of the nineteenth century. New surprises await us there, and we can only shake our heads and offer our gratitude one more time to the God of all surprises, and for the grace that is His instrument.

Here is that story.

The Woman Who Started the War

Harriet Beecher Stowe wanted to be a writer, and she was off to a reasonable start. She and her sister published a children's book that enjoyed modest success. But Harriet wanted to write novels like Dickens and Hawthorne. What she needed most was a subject worthy of a writer's passion.

Harriet lived with her husband in Cincinnati, Ohio, where her father was the president of Lane Theological Seminary. Cincinnati was an interesting town in 1850—a frontier town, really. It thrived on the characters and commerce of the Ohio River.

It was in this setting that Harriet began to meet fugitive slaves who had escaped captivity in the South. Cincinnati was an important stop on the Underground Railroad, by which many African-Americans were able to come northward to freedom.

Harriet met some of the former slaves, saw their scars, and heard their stories. With her husband, she also visited a few Southern towns and witnessed the ugly realities of plantation life with her own eyes. She couldn't cleanse those sights from her mind even after the Stowes moved to Maine. To add even greater drama to the situation, the Fugitive Slave Law was passed in 1850, making it a crime to harbor a runaway slave. Harriet Beecher Stowe felt more and more indignant over the injustice of this whole establishment. So did many other people. Slavery was America's great burning issue.

Yet it was the loss of her son Charley that finally provided the spark that moved Harriet's pen. Her baby died of cholera, and she grieved miserably. Now she understood what it was like when slave women had their newborn children ripped from their arms and taken away from them forever. Now she felt an emotional link to the American slave.

Her novel *Uncle Tom's Cabin* was published in 1852. More than any mere speech or tract, it would be this sensational book that would personalize the issue of slavery for many Americans. Readers knew Uncle Tom and Simon Legree as if they were real people. Many folks had simply thought the existence of the industry was unfortunate; now they were moved and impassioned.

The antislavery movement had grown in power from its origins in England, where men like John Newton had lit the candles that would grow into flame under William Wilberforce and his associates. In America, Harriet Beecher Stowe's novel spread the same fire. Within a few years, the American Civil War would be fought over this issue. Abraham Lincoln would later meet the author, who was now a celebrity, and joke, "So you're the little woman who wrote the book that started this great war."

One other factor lay behind the phenomenal success of *Uncle Tom's Cabin.* "I could not control the story; the Lord himself wrote it," she would say later. "I was but an instrument in His hands, and to Him should be given all the praise." Even in the emotional devastation of losing her child, she found that God's grace was sufficient. She channeled her mourning into heartfelt writing and allowed the Lord to use her gifts.

Harriet Beecher Stowe's novel tells the story of a Christian slave who is sold to Simon Legree. He has taught himself to read the Bible, but his new master allows no free time for his slaves. Legree demands that Tom deny his faith and live for the devil. Tom replies, "I'll hold on. The Lord may help me, or not help me; but I'll hold to Him and believe Him to the last."

This determination inspires Legree to new levels of cruelty. Tom weakens under the constant barrage of his master but holds on to his faith with his last reserves of courage. Then one night he sits at a dying fire, deep in despair, when a vision rises before him: "One crowned with thorns, buffeted, bleeding." The suffering slave looks into the eyes of his true Master and draws strength from the grace and power of the vision. Before his eyes, the thorns are transformed into rays of heavenly glory. The figure bends closer to Tom and encourages him with the promise of heaven for those who overcome as He, the Lord, has overcome.

The vision fades and Tom is suddenly awake, and "the triumphant words of a hymn" fill the silence of the night. He remembers the song from happier days and begins to sing. His melody happens to be three verses of "Amazing Grace." The first two come from Newton's "lost verses," the ones we seldom use today.

The slave's third verse, however, is the charm:

When we've been there ten thousand years,
Bright shining as the sun . . .

Tom is a changed man now. He gives up any idea of physical freedom and embraces the eternal freedom that is his legacy as a follower of Christ. He devotes himself wholeheartedly to sharing this hope in Christ with his fellow slaves. The outcome is not hard to foresee. Simon Legree has Tom whipped to death, and the slave joins His Savior in the ultimate fellowship, where a crown of glory awaits those who finish the race.

There has always been power in the idea of martyrdom, even when the martyr is a fictional character like Uncle Tom. Every reader knew that Harriet Beecher Stowe's Uncle Tom represented many thousands of genuine slaves who were not fictional at all. In the early church, it was said that "the blood of the martyrs is seed." What grows from that seed? Faith—passionate faith. And a faith that gets to work. A decade after the publication of Stowe's novel, slavery was outlawed and Christian activism had taken the lead in its defeat.

This is the first use of the final verse of "Amazing Grace" that can be found. Most scholars believe that it was *Uncle Tom's Cabin*, therefore, that finished the work that John Newton had done; it was the book that inspired America to take a stand against slavery, just as Newton, through Wilberforce, had done in England. This is the triumphant path of grace that begins at the foot of the cross and leads to the present day, and to *you*.

What path will grace follow now, through your commitment and your gratitude?

The Fragrance of Grace

Amazing grace is the thread that ties together the powerful, righteous work of outlawing slavery in two great nations: amazing grace as the miraculous work of the Spirit, and "Amazing Grace" as an enduring hymn of gratitude for the love and mercy of God, given freely to those who might have died without hope.

Grace taught Newton's heart to fear, and grace his fears relieved. Grace taught his heart to see the reality of justice beyond the social conventions of his day. It inspired him to write words that for many generations would perfectly capture that grace as it had first captured him.

Grace taught Harriet Beecher Stowe's heart to grieve for the weary, abused human beings she met in Cincinnati. It strengthened her to survive her own grieving over an infant son taken by disease and to glorify God regardless of circumstances. Finally, that same grace inspired her to write a classic novel that would complement Newton's classic hymn—which she ended in a new way, to complete the circle of God's providence.

In her book *Radical Gratitude,* Ellen Vaughn tells about an incident that took place on the Washington subway system. The crowded train had stalled on an underground track. Harried commuters were beside themselves. No one had been speaking to anyone, but now they burst into mutual, frenzied bouts of accusation against the driver, the Metro authorities, the federal government, or anyone else they could blame for this terrible inconvenience.

Somewhere in the midst of all this invective, a woman with a number of bulky shopping bags dropped and shattered a new bottle of perfume. Within a few minutes, the pure, luxurious fragrance had wafted the length of the crowded car. It was as if the fresh smell released people from a dark spell. They breathed in, grinned with pleasure, relaxed, and began laughing with each other.[5]

This world, filled with complaints, threats, and cries of despair, could use a whiff of the aroma of paradise. The darkness may seem impermeable, yet it flees before the light of God's grace. All we need is to find our own voice. Grace will make use of the letters of Paul, the lyrics of Newton, the literature of Mrs. Stowe, or the love that is yours exclusively to express. His grace can take any and every form. It can burst out in any hopeless or desperate situation. It has traveled its mysterious path for two thousand years, and this present darkness can do nothing but afford it a greater opportunity for God's greater glory.

I pray that you are even now following the path of God's fragrant and beautiful grace, that it is filling your heart with a peace and joy that stand defiant against the worst attacks of the evil one, that your relationships are constantly becoming more and more Christlike, so that those who know you cannot help but be touched by grace and cannot help but ask about its source. I pray that even as you have been captured by grace, you will be its vessel for helping it capture more and more of a world desperate to know it; so that one day, when we stand before the Source of amazing grace, you'll have even greater reason for joy and gratitude, for in the end you became part of the story yourself.

Freely you have received, freely give.

—JESUS (MATTHEW 10:8)

Moments of Grace

Here are four ideas for cultivating thankfulness. First, count your blessings—literally. The hymnist Frances Ridley Havergal (author of "Take My Life and Let It Be") kept a daily thanksgiving list along with her prayer list, and each day she recorded new blessings for which to be thankful. Why not give that a try? You might use your daily calendar or handheld computer. Have you ever thanked God for the small, overlooked blessings? Hot water in the mornings? A warm pair of socks? Your shoes?

Second, ask a close friend to tell you when you complain. Most of us gripe and complain so frequently it's become a habit of which we're unaware. Appoint a friend as an attitude spotter.

Third, begin using biblical terminology when thanking others. Instead of saying, "Thank you," try, "I thank God for you."

Fourth, make it a habit to go to sleep every night with thanksgiving on your mind. When you turn out the lights, find three or four blessings and let your last waking thoughts be contented thanksgiving prayers of praise to God.

Captured Forever

I f you've read this far, my friend, then you and I have become travel companions of a sort.

Together we've come through the storms with John Newton and then sat beside him at the hearth and marveled at the transformation of his spirit. We've wondered how it is that a person who begins life as a social castaway—bereft of mother, abandoned by father, and abused by his fellow men—can become so loving and find such inexhaustibly gracious resources to offer the world.

You and I have also walked a few miles with a man once known as Saul. We have watched as he rooted Christians out of their homes. We have observed his ironclad views of religious purity—and seen all of it disappear into the dust of one Damascus Road. Maybe there were times when you placed the book aside just to sit and contemplate the impossibility of these things: a man with gold-plated credentials as a Hebrew rabbi, a Greek scholar, and a Roman citizen, pushing all of it aside for a life of hardship, telling everyone about the crucified carpenter from Nazareth, knowing it could only lead to his own execution. Why?

If it were only about John Newton or Paul the apostle, perhaps we could dismiss these things as freak occurrences of history. But we know better than that, don't we? We know that their living church has conquered million-to-one odds to survive and topple the Roman Empire in those first years. It has withstood political suppression, intellectual attack, and social upheaval on every populated continent. It begins with a crucified peasant and a handful of unimpressive followers; it ends with hundreds of millions of devout believers alive today. How?

And now, at this very moment, that living faith has found its way to the doorway of your own heart.

You and I have navigated these pages together, it's true. But there was always a Third Party in our presence. You sensed it, didn't you? John Newton knew He was there. Paul knew He was there. And now He stands before you and asks about your own acknowledgment.

This is where my personal part of your journey ends. Our paths diverge here, for there is only One who can make that final leg of the journey—the one that leads into your soul. I know that's what He longs to do today. As in Francis Thompson's poem, the tracks of the Hound of Heaven have followed you to the present moment, the present situation, the present point of decision. Jesus Christ, the very personification of grace, loves you deeply. He has loved you since before you were born. According to the Bible, He has anticipated this moment with longing, ever since the foundation of time. He has been anxious to know you as His friend. That's how much you mean to Him.

I want to be certain you know exactly what is involved in saying yes to that love and that grace. There's nothing complicated about it, believe me. There are no requirements you need to go out into the world and fulfill. There's not a cent that you need to pay. It's all about grace, remember?

You simply need to agree with Jesus Christ that only He can calm the storms of life. You need only to take your stand beside Him as He stands beside you, to let *Him* answer for every sin and failing in your life.

Then begins the life of joy that He has always wanted for you. As we discussed, it's not a life free of pain or struggle. But it's a life with Him by your side, Him giving you hope, Him giving you all that you need to come through any storm. It also means an eternity of enjoying His presence. Think of that, my friend—an eternity in which there will be no more pain, no more tears, and you will finally be all that He created you to be.

The reward is unfathomable; the requirement is simple. How, then, can you say yes to Jesus Christ right here and now?

1. *Acknowledge* that you are a helpless sinner, like every one of us in this world. As Paul writes, "There is none righteous, no, not one" (Romans 3:10).

2. *Affirm* that Jesus Christ, being God's perfect and sinless Son, accepted your own penalty by dying for you. "But God demonstrates His own love toward us, in that while we were still sinners, Christ died for us" (Romans 5:8).

3. *Ask* Him to save you right now. "If you confess with your mouth the Lord Jesus and believe in your heart that God has raised Him from the dead, you will be saved" (Romans 10:9).

4. *Always* serve Jesus Christ as Lord and Master, every day. "But you are not in the flesh but in the Spirit, if indeed the Spirit of God dwells in you" (Romans 8:9).

Yes, this decision will totally transform your life. From that very moment when you accept the salvation and lordship of Christ, He will begin to transform you a bit more every day to resemble Himself. You will become wiser, stronger, more of a blessing to others. But all of it begins with that one simple statement—that one sincere *yes*, from your heart to the heart of Christ.

If you're not sure exactly how to go about it, I would suggest that you imagine Jesus Christ right there in your presence, as He most certainly is. Then say a simple prayer, which means nothing more than talking to Him. Your words might be like these:

Lord Jesus, I'm like everyone else—I can't make it through life on my own. I'm imperfect. I'm prone to sin. I have come to realize that there's nothing in the world I can do to make myself acceptable to You. But I know that You loved me so much that You were willing to submit to the cross on my behalf. That's a grace so amazing I cannot understand it; I can only accept it. And I do. I accept Your free gift, and I know that from this moment on, I am saved. I am a child of heaven. And I give the rest of my life to serving You and experiencing the joy that only You offer. Fill me now, dear Lord, and raise me to walk in newness of life. I thank You and praise You! Amen.

If you have become a child of Christ through this book, I congratulate you and welcome you with all my heart! Life for you truly begins right now—could anything be more exciting? I hope the first thing you do is to let someone know about your wonderful decision. Find a good church where Christ is preached and where your fellow believers will care for you and help you grow.

I would love to hear about your experience too. It would add joy to my day. You can get in touch with me by writing to:

Turning Point Ministries
P.O. Box 3838
San Diego, CA 92163

My friend, may your life reflect the grace that is too marvelous for words. May you begin now to partake of it wholeheartedly, from this moment until we arrive together at that final destination, where you and I will bow before the Author of grace, and where all of His love and all of His mercy will reach their ultimate expression.

SELECT BIBLIOGRAPHY

Bull, Josiah. *"But Now I See": The Life of John Newton.* Carlisle, PA: Banner of Truth Trust, 1998.

Cecil, Richard. *The Life of John Newton,* ed. Marylynn Rouse. Fearn, Ross-shire: Christian Focus, 2000.

Hindmarsh, D. Bruce. *John Newton and the English Evangelical Tradition.* Grand Rapids: Eerdmans, 2000.

Newton, John. *The Journal of a Slave Trader: 1750-1754.* ed. with introduction by Bernard Martin and Mark Spurrell. London: Epworth, n.d.

————. *Letters.* Carlisle, PA: Banner of Truth Trust, 1960.

————. *Letters and Reflections to My Adopted Daughters.* Comp. Jody Moreen. Enumclaw, WA: Pleasant Word, 2005.

————. *The Life and Spirituality of John Newton,* introduction by D. Bruce Hindmarsh. Vancouver, B.C.: Regent College Publishing, 2003.

————. *Out of the Depths.* Revised for Today's Readers by Dennis R. Hillman. Grand Rapids: Kregel, 2003.

————. *The Searcher of Hearts.* Fearn, Ross-shire; Christian Focus, 1997.

————. *Thoughts upon the African Slave Trade.* London: 1883.

Turner, Steve. *Amazing Grace.* New York: HarperCollins, 2002.

NOTES

Chapter I: The Captivating Presence of Grace

1. "A Moment of Grace." www.nytimes.com./2005/08/17/opinion.
2. D. Bruce Hindmarsh, *John Newton and the English Evangelical Tradition* (Grand Rapids: Eerdmans, 1996), 51.
3. John Newton, *Out of the Depths*, revised by Dennis R. Hillman (Grand Rapids: Kregel, 2003), 28, 33, 41, 66.
4. Richard Cecil, *The Life of John Newton*, ed. Marylynn Rouse (Fearn, Ross-shire: Christian Focus, 2000), 162.
5. Quoted in Steve Turner, *Amazing Grace* (New York: Harper-Collins, 2002), 215.
6. Ibid., 217.
7. Ibid.
8. Ibid., 218.
9. D. M. Lloyd-Jones, *Romans: An Exposition of Chapters 3:20–4:25, Atonement and Justification* (Grand Rapids: Zondervan, 1970), 57.
10. W. H. Griffith Thomas, *Outline Studies in the Acts of the Apostles* (Grand Rapids: Eerdmans, 1956).
11. Victor Hugo, *Les Miserablés*, Trans. Isabel Florence Hapgood. In the public domain. www.gutenberg.org/etext/135.

Chapter 2: The Compassionate Plan of Grace

1. Thomas G. Long, "God Be Merciful to Me, a Miscalculator," *Theology Today*, vol. 50, no. 2 (July 1993), 165–68.

2. John Newton, *The Life and Spirituality of John Newton*, introduction by D. Bruce Hindmarsh (Vancouver, B.C.: Regent College Publishing, 2003), 50.

3. Cornelius Plantinga Jr., *Not The Way It's Supposed to Be: A Breviary of Sin* (Grand Rapids: Eerdmans, 1995), 199.

4. Charles R. Swindoll, *Growing Deep in the Christian Life* (Portland: Multnomah, 1986), 207.

5. Kent Hughes, *Romans—Righteousness from Heaven* (Wheaton, IL: Crossway, 1991), 76.

6. Aleksandr Solzhenitsyn, *The Gulag Archipelago 1918–1956: An Experiment in Literary Investigation* (Boulder, CO: Westview, 1973), 168.

7. Donald Grey Barnhouse, *God's Remedy, God's River—Romans*, vol. II (Grand Rapids: Eerdmans, 1953), 5–6.

8. John R. W. Stott, *The Cross of Christ* (Downer's Grove, IL: InterVarsity, 1986), 189–92.

9. Benjamin Breckinridge Warfield, "Redeemer, Redemption" in *The Person and Work of Christ* (Philadelphia: Presbyterian and Reformed Publishing, 1950), 325–48.

10. James Montgomery Boice, *Romans, Vol. I—Justification by Faith: Romans 1–4* (Grand Rapids: Baker, 1991), 375–76.

11. William Cowper, *The Works of William Cowper* (London: H. G. Bohn, 1853), 101.

12. Richard Cecil, *The Life of John Newton*, ed. Marylynn Rouse (Fearn, Ross-shire: Christian Focus, 2000), 119.

13. John Piper, "Insanity and Spiritual Songs in the Soul of the Saint: Reflections on the Life of William Cowper," Bethlehem Conference for Pastors, 29 January 1992. http://www.desiringgod.org/library/biographies/92cowper.html.

Chapter 3: The Converting Power of Grace

1. Henri J. M. Nouwen, *The Return of the Prodigal: A Story of Homecoming* (New York: Doubleday, 1992).
2. Kenneth E. Bailey, *The Cross and the Prodigal* (Downers Grove, IL: InterVarsity, 2005), 52–53.
3. Ibid., 67.
4. Ibid.

Chapter 4: The Clear Perspective of Grace

1. Josiah Bull, *"But Now I See": The Life of John Newton* (Carlisle, PA: Banner of Truth Trust, 1998), 62, 358.
2. Cornelius Plantinga Jr., *Not the Way It's Supposed to Be: A Breviary of Sin* (Grand Rapids: Eerdmans, 1995), xiii.
3. Mark R. McMinn, *Why Sin Matters: The Surprising Relationship Between Our Sin and God's Grace* (Wheaton, IL: Tyndale, 2004), 21.
4. Ibid., 50.
5. Donald Grey Barnhouse, *Man's Ruin, God's Wrath—Romans*, vol. I (Grand Rapids: Eerdmans. 1959), 18.
6. Adapted from Charles Haddon Spurgeon, *Earnest Expostulations in Metropolitan Tabernacle Pulpit*, vol. 29 (Carlisle, PA: The Banner of Truth Trust, 1971), 196.
7. William Hendriksen, *New Testament Commentary: Exposition of Paul's Epistle to the Romans* (Grand Rapids: Baker, 1980), 95.
8. C. S. Lewis, *Mere Christianity* (New York: Macmillan, 1958), 4–5.
9. John Warwick Montgomery, *Damned Through the Church* (Minneapolis: Bethany Fellowship, 1970), 62–63.

10. Adapted from Kent Hughes, *Romans—Righteousness from Heaven* (Wheaton, IL: Crossway, 1991), 71–72.

Chapter 5: The Comforting Provision of Grace

1. John R. W. Stott, *Romans: God's Good News for the World* (Downers Grove, IL: InterVarsity, 1994), 140.
2. Lloyd Ogilvie, *Drumbeat of Love* (Waco, TX: Word, 1978), 176–77.
3. W. H. Griffith Thomas, *Outline Studies in the Acts of the Apostles* (Grand Rapids: Eerdmans, 1956), 150.

Chapter 6: The Connecting Point of Grace

1. John Newton, *The Life and Spirituality of John Newton*, introduction by D. Bruce Hindmarsh (Vancouver, B.C.: Regent College Publishing, 2003), 54.
2. Ibid., 57.
3. Ibid., 63.
4. D. Bruce Hindmarsh, *John Newton and the English Evangelical Tradition* (Grand Rapids: Eerdmans, 2000), 13.
5. W. H. Griffith Thomas, *Outline Studies in the Acts of the Apostles* (Grand Rapids: Eerdmans, 1956), 163.
6. C. S. Lewis, *Christian Reflections* (San Diego: Harcourt Brace, 1956), 228.
7. F. B. Meyer, *Paul: A Servant of Jesus Christ* (Fort Washington, PA: Christian Literature Crusade, 1978), 42.
8. C. S. Lewis, *Surprised by Joy* (San Diego: Harcourt Brace, 1956), 228.

Chapter 7: The Confusing Paradox of Grace

1. Mrs. Charles Cowman, *Streams in the Desert* (Grand Rapids: Zondervan, 1965), 90.
2. Kenneth Wuest, *Wuest's Word Studies from the Greek New Testament*, vol. 3 (Grand Rapids: Eerdmans, 1973), 82.
3. Paul Lee Tan, *Encyclopedia of 7000 Illustrations: A Treasury of Illustrations, Anecdotes, Facts, and Quotations for Pastors, Teachers, and Christian Workers*, electronic ed. (Garland, TX: Bible Communications, 1979). Published in electronic form by Logos Research Systems, 1997.
4. John Newton, *Out of the Depths*, revised by Dennis R. Hillman (Grand Rapids: Kregel, 2003), 12.
5. "August 15, 1964—Congo Rebels Reached Helen Roseveare," Christian History Institute. http://chi/gospelcom.net/DAILYF/2002/08/daily-08-15-2002.shtml.
6. "Digging Ditches: Evangelicals Now Interviews Legendary Missionary Helen Roseveare." www.e-n.org.uk/2005-09/3132-Digging-ditches.htm.
7. Josiah Bull, *"But Now I See": The Life of John Newton* (Carlisle, PA: Banner of Truth Trust, 1998), 304.

Chapter 8: The Confident Promise of Grace

1. John MacArthur, *The MacArthur New Testament Commentary: Romans 1–8* (Chicago: Moody, 1991), 471.
2. John Phillips, *Exploring Romans* (Chicago: Moody, 1969), 134.
3. Donald Grey Barnhouse, *Romans, God's Heirs: Romans 8:1–39* (Grand Rapids: Eerdmans, 1959), 153.

4. Annie Johnson Flint, quoted in Mrs. Charles Cowman, *Streams in the Desert* (Grand Rapids: Zondervan, 1965), 110–11.

5. chi/gospelcom.net/DAILYF/2002/08.

6. www.e-n.org.uk/2005-09/3132-DiggingDitches.htm.

7. John Newton, *Letters and Reflections to My Adopted Daughters*, comp. Jody Moreen (Enumclaw, WA: Pleasant Word, 2005), 105.

Chapter 9: The Compelling Prospect of Grace

1. Steve Turner, *Amazing Grace* (New York: Harper Collins, 2002), 107.

2. Josiah Bull, *"But Now I See": The Life of John Newton* (Carlisle: Banner of Truth Trust, 1998), 359.

Chapter 10: The Continual Praise of Grace

1. James MacDonald, *Lord, Change My Attitude (Before It's Too Late)* (Chicago: Moody, 2001), 35.

2. Robert A. Emmons and Michael E. McCullough, "Highlights from the Research Project on Gratitude and Thankfulness." http://psychology.ucdavis.edu/labs/emmons/.

3. www.sermonillustrator.org/illustrator/sermon2/blessed.htm.

4. James S. Spiegel, *How to Be Good in a World Gone Bad: Living a Life of Christian Virtue* (Grand Rapids: Kregel, 2004), 174.

5. Ellen Vaughn, *Radical Gratitude* (Grand Rapids: Zondervan, 2005), 48.

Let David Jeremiah help you be
CAPTURED BY GRACE.

Embark on your
Pathway to Grace today!

STEP
I

Log on to

www.CapturedByGrace.com

and access your FREE

Pathway to Grace Guide.

This downloadable resource connects

you to an exhaustive list of Scripture

that leads you through God's plan of

grace, forgiveness, salvation,

and dynamic Christian living!

STEP 2

Create a reading plan to help you systematically read through *Captured by Grace*. Read and study at your own pace.

Spend 10 weeks reading *Captured by Grace*. Read one chapter each week and slowly unravel the comfort and peace of God's unwavering love. As you journey through the lyrics of John Newton's hymn "Amazing Grace," you will see that God's gift of grace is offered for the past, the present, and the future.

You will find "Moments of Grace" sections at the end of each chapter. Take the time to read these special personal application pages and commit to taking the call-to-action steps suggested.

When you incorporate acts of grace into your daily life, you will discover how you can be more fully captured by God's grace.

EQUIP YOURSELF FOR THE JOURNEY

Add any of these fine *Captured by Grace* resources by
David Jeremiah to your personal growth library:

STEP 3

CBGCDAL

CBGSG

CBGJ

Captured by Grace
Audio Message Album 10 CD Messages

Captured by Grace is all about the multifaceted
jewel of grace: the past, present, and future of
the Christian experience. In this teaching series,
Dr. David Jeremiah reveals less familiar aspects
of grace such as its plan, power, promise, and
prospect—as well as the paradox of grace.
If your Christian life is not what you know it
could and should be, it may be lacking grace.

Album includes all ten audio *Captured by Grace*
messages by Dr. Jeremiah on compact disc.
(Book was adapted from these messages.)

Captured by Grace
Study Guide & Workbook

This 128-page study resource correlates with
the *Captured by Grace* book and audio teaching
series. Each lesson provides an outline, over-
view, application, and study questions for each
chapter or message.

The lessons in this study guide are suitable for
personal or group studies.

Captured by Grace
Journal

Ten interactive chapters correlate to each
chapter of David Jeremiah's *Captured by Grace*
book. Delve deeper into the abundance of
God's grace by searching the Scriptures,
recording your thoughts and prayers, and
keeping a record of your personal journey
to grace.